Mediaeval Studies
The Annmary Brown Memorial
Box 19 5
Brown University
Providence, RI   02912

THE
Sutton Hoo Ship Burial
A HANDBOOK

THE
Sutton Hoo
Ship Burial
A HANDBOOK

RUPERT
BRUCE-MITFORD
MA, Hon D Litt (Dublin), FBA, FSA,
FSA Scot

*Formerly Keeper of Medieval and Later Antiquities
in the British Museum*

PUBLISHED FOR
THE TRUSTEES OF THE BRITISH MUSEUM
BY BRITISH MUSEUM PUBLICATIONS LIMITED

© 1972; 1979, The Trustees of the British Museum

First edition (*Provisional Guide*) 1947
Fifth impression (revised) 1956
Tenth impression 1966
New edition (*Handbook*) 1968
Second edition (*Handbook*) 1972
Third edition (*Handbook*) 1979

ISBN 0 7141 1343 3 (cased)
ISBN 0 7141 1344 1 (paper)

Published by British Museum Publications Ltd
6 Bedford Square, London WC1B 3RA

British Library Cataloguing in Publication Data

Bruce-Mitford, Rupert
    The Sutton Hoo ship burial: A Handbook.—3rd ed.
    1. Ship burial   2. Anglo-Saxons
    3. Suffolk, Eng.—Antiquities
    I. Title   II. British Museum
    942.6′46   GT3380

DESIGNED BY CRAIG DODD

Set in Ehrhardt medium Roman (453)

Printed in Great Britain by
Butler & Tanner Ltd Frome and London

Contents

PREFACE TO THE THIRD EDITION

There have been several new developments since the second edition went to press. The most important is the new reconstruction of the shield, which replaces that made in 1946. The aspect of the shield has been changed by the addition of new features applied in gold foil, by alterations to the shape of the bird on the front, including the recovery of the decorative designs of its tail and wing, and by the attachment of the loose 'sword ring' (p. 33) to the shield. The location of every feature on the front of the shield, apart from its central boss and the peripheral animal heads, has also been changed. These alterations, based on internal evidence, make it possible for the first time to assess correctly the shield's archaeological context.

Other developments include the making of a striking and accurate modern version of the helmet, by armourers in the Tower of London, using electrotypes of the facial features and bronze decorative sheeting supplied by the British Museum. It recreates something of the quality and impact once possessed by the original (22, 34). The two large drinking-horns have been rebuilt so that their mounts are fitted on horn-shapes of the correct dimensions (42, 43). Another notable change is the replacement of the 1940 versions of the lines of the ship and of its structural details (this latter incorrect in many respects) by an authoritative new ship-plan (70). The 'scramasax' referred to consistently in the literature is now, thanks to an observation by Miss Angela Care Evans, correctly identified as a spearhead. There have also been minor adjustments to the text bibliography.

I am very glad to take this opportunity of acknowledging the fine work of Mr Nigel Williams, the Conservation Officer responsible for building the new shield, who also collaborated with the craftsmen of the Royal Armouries in the Tower in the production of the modern version of the helmet, having been himself chiefly responsible for the new helmet reconstruction of 1971, exhibited beside the modern version. I am indebted to Mrs Susan Youngs, MA, Research Assistant in the Sutton Hoo unit, for preparing this new edition of the Handbook.

The British Museum   RUPERT BRUCE-MITFORD

LIST OF ILLUSTRATIONS

Where not otherwise acknowledged, photographs are by the British Museum's Photographic Studio. Most of the figures are drawn by official illustrators on the staff of the Museum, Mr C. O. Waterhouse, MBE, Miss M. O. Miller and Mr Eric Eden.

Frontispiece: General views of the excavated ship, with work in progress (Miss B. Wagstaff, ARPS)

THE Sutton Hoo Ship Burial

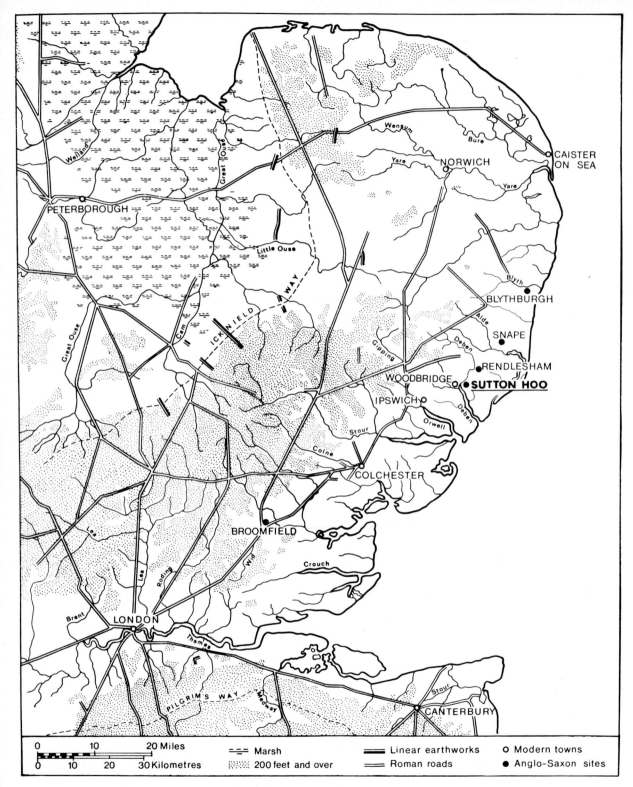

1 *Map of the East Anglian region, including places mentioned in the text.*
(Based on the Ordnance Survey Maps of Roman Britain and the Dark Ages
by permission of the Controller of HM Stationery Office.)

CHAPTER I

Discovery

At Woodbridge the tidal estuary of the River Deben runs roughly north and south (*1*). Between the estuary and the sea, some six miles to the east, there lay in 1939 an ancient expanse of sandy heathland, covered with turf and bracken, one of the largest surviving areas of heath in Suffolk. A good deal of this has since been taken into cultivation. On this heathland, at Sutton Hoo, National Grid Reference TM 288487, opposite the small town of Woodbridge, lies a sizeable group of ancient burial mounds, or barrows. They are situated on the 100 ft contour, at the crest of an escarpment overlooking the tidal waters of the estuary, and are at least fifteen in number (*2*). Before the planting of its slopes in the nineteenth century the escarpment was bare. Several of the barrows, and particularly the ship-barrow, standing forward a little on a spur between two coombes, would have been visible from the river. Today, at high tide, they are almost half a mile inland. When the Anglo-Saxon burial ground was in use in the sixth and seventh centuries AD, before sea-walls were built to confine the tidal waters, the barrows must still have been a good 600 yards from high water, a long haul for a large boat.

In 1938, the late Mrs Edith May Pretty, JP, on whose estate all but one of the barrows as yet recognized were situated, decided to investigate their contents. In that year three were accordingly opened, the work being carried out by a local excavator and antiquary, Mr Basil Brown, employed by Mrs Pretty, the Ipswich Museum having a general surveillance.[1] The three mounds revealed an interesting mixture of burial practices. Two (nos. 3 and 4; *2*) contained cremations, one (no. 3) being apparently intact and one (no. 4) ransacked. The third (no. 2), the largest mound on the site (see p. 71), had contained an inhumed burial that had been deposited in a small boat, apparently with one end cut off, perhaps originally 25 ft (8 m) long; but this burial too had been ransacked and the boat almost entirely destroyed. Only seven rivets, out of some forty recovered, were actually found undisturbed in alignments. The

Overleaf, left:
2 Plan of the Sutton Hoo site, based on fresh surveys carried out in 1965–66. Mound 1, which covered the great ship-burial is shown in the excavated state, with associated dumps, in which it remained from 1939 until excavation was continued in 1965. Mounds 2, 3 and 4 were excavated in 1938. Clearly defined tumuli are shown in heavy hachures. Further possible tumuli are indicated by lighter hachures. Modern features of the site are shown and identified.

Overleaf, right:
3 Stag figure in bronze (Scale, 2/1)

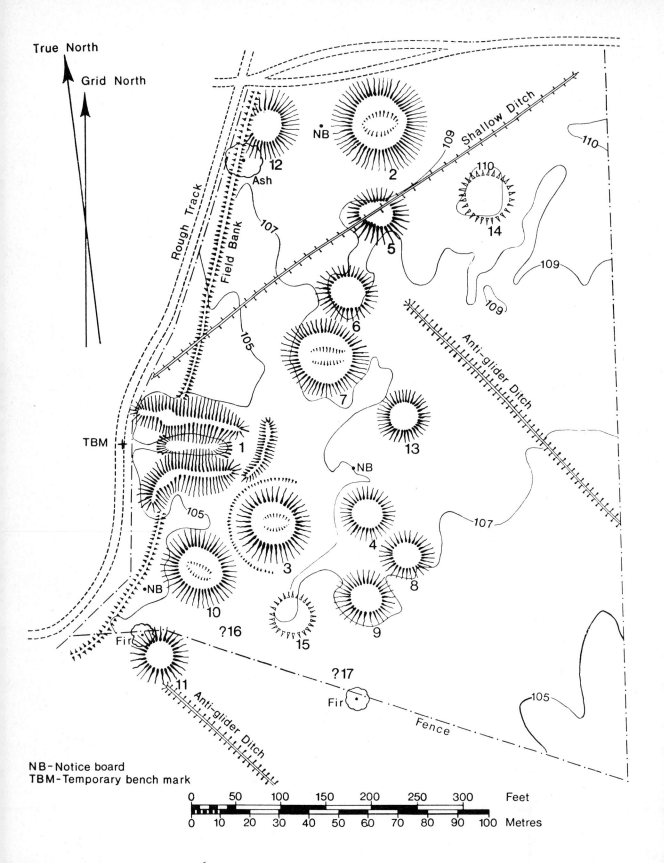

True North

Grid North

Rough Track

Field Bank

Ash

12

NB

2

109 Shallow Ditch

110

110

14

109

109

109

107

105

5

6

7

Anti-glider Ditch

13

NB

TBM

1

105

107

3

4

8

NB

10

9

15

Fir

?16

11

Anti-glider Ditch

?17

Fir

Fence

105

NB – Notice board
TBM – Temporary bench mark

| 0 | 50 | 100 | 150 | 200 | 250 | 300 | Feet |

| 0 | 10 | 20 | 30 | 40 | 50 | 60 | 70 | 80 | 90 | 100 | Metres |

finds from the three mounds were few and mere fragments, yet enough to indicate considerable status for these dead and to show unusual features. Finds made in Mound 2 (the boatgrave) included the point of a pattern-welded sword, an ornamental fragment from a shield, fragments of a silver-gilt foil mount with stamped animal ornament which proved to be identical with one of the dies (*43b*) used in the decoration of the aurochs' horns found in the following year; and parts of a small, dark-blue glass bowl of a special type so far found only in England and Norway, and probably made in Kent.[2] Finds from Mound 3 (an apparently intact cremation) included a portion of an imported hardstone plaque of Classical or Early Byzantine origin, finely carved with part of a winged figure, probably a Victory; the small bronze lid of an imported vessel, probably of eastern Mediterranean origin and either of late Roman or Byzantine date; and an iron axe-head. The third (no. 4) yielded remains of a thin bronze bowl in which the gathered-up remains of the cremation had evidently been interred, with traces of textile adhering to the bronze fragments; and a small undecorated bone gaming-counter, flat on one side and convex on the other. All these finds were presented to Ipswich Museum by Mrs Pretty.

In 1939, Mrs Pretty, encouraged by Mr Guy Maynard, then Curator of the Ipswich Museum, decided to continue the work and to open the tallest of the barrows, said to be standing to a height of some 9 feet (for further discussion of the features of the ship-barrow, see p. 71). The excavation was begun by Mr Brown, who cut into the mound from the east or landward side and soon came upon a system of rusted iron rivets in position. These he immediately recognized, from his 1938 experience, as belonging to a boat which, it soon became evident, must be of considerable size. Mr Brown freed the whole of what proved to be the bows of the ship of its overburden of barrow material down to the old ground level, removing also some of the sand that had been filled into the ship. He reached the centre of the ship, where a burial might be expected, and there, in trial excavations, exposed tantalizing pieces of bronze, wood and iron. It was evident that the ship must be of great size and must project well outside the limits of the barrow as it then stood.

In view of the experience of 1938, and especially as others of the barrows, in addition to those excavated in 1938, showed clear signs of having been opened by treasure-hunters, it was hardly expected that an intact burial-deposit would be found. The excavators realized, however, that at any rate something complex and important lay beneath. A halt was wisely called, and the British Museum and the Inspectorate of Ancient Monuments of HM Office of Works (now the Department of the Environment) were asked for advice as to future procedure. As a result, work was continued under the direction of Mr C. W. Phillips, FSA, at

4 *Enamelled circular escutcheon with* millefiore *glass insets and adjacent boar's head escutcheon; from the rim of the large hanging bowl.* (*Scale, 2/1*)

5   *Archaeologists in the burial-chamber area. Above, Basil Brown, with below, left to right, Grahame Clark, W. F. Grimes, Mrs Margaret Guido and Stuart Piggott.*

the time a Fellow of Selwyn College, Cambridge, and Secretary of the Prehistoric Society, a very able excavator, who was fortunately able to gather together on the spur of the moment a team of highly skilled assistants (5).[3]

The task that confronted them was one of unprecedented difficulty. No one in this country had ever excavated a burial deposit remotely approaching this in importance or complexity and no one had ever, apart from the recovery of prehistoric dug-out canoes from river mud, excavated a ship, especially one whose timbers had wholly disappeared. The great size of the ship, of which clear traces remained in the ground (*frontispiece*), led the excavators to suppose that the burial was that of a Viking and contemporaneous with the well-known Viking ship-burials of the ninth and tenth centuries at Oseberg and Gokstad in Norway,[4] or Ladby in Denmark,[5] or some of lesser interest known from the Isle of Man. It soon became apparent, however, that the burial belonged to an earlier age and was of a kind unparalleled in British archaeology. During the last week in July, gold jewellery, coins, silver plate, weapons and armour, the remains of cauldrons, buckets and dishes of bronze and iron, textiles, leather, cups, drinking-horns and miscellaneous other objects were uncovered from what had been a burial chamber amidships. It was the richest treasure ever dug from British soil, and the most important archaeological document yet found in Europe for the era of the migrations of the Germanic peoples (fifth to seventh centuries AD) in which the settlement of England variously by the Angles and Saxons, with an admixture of Frisians, Franks and Jutes, was an episode.

On 14 August 1939 a Coroner's inquest was held to decide whether the objects found were Treasure Trove, and so Crown property. The Coroner found that they were not Treasure Trove, and they were therefore the property of the landowner, Mrs Pretty. On Wednesday, 23 August, it was announced that Mrs Pretty, with very great generosity and wisdom, had presented the whole of the find to the Nation.

Three days later, the work of the excavators in removing the last remains of the burial deposit and completing the study of the ship was brought to a close. There was time for first-aid treatment of fragile objects and perishables in the British Museum laboratory, and for the finds to be listed and deposited in safety, before war broke out.

6 *The burial-chamber area before any of the objects had been removed.*

CHAPTER II

The burial deposit

The account of the excavations which follows is based on that of Mr C. W. Phillips, published in *Antiquaries Journal*, XX, 1940, with minor revisions in the light of subsequent work on the finds and study of the records.

A general view of the area of the burial chamber in process of excavation (*6*), shows it before any of the objects that had constituted the burial deposit had been lifted. The manner in which the objects and groups of objects were laid out is illustrated in *7*. They had been placed roughly in the form of an H, with lines of objects ranged across the ship against the east and west walls of the burial chamber and a series joining them down the centre of the ship, laid out along the keel line. The ship had been drawn up from the estuary bow first and buried with the bows pointing inland, and the stern to the water. The objects as found lay directly on the ship's bottom, or nearly so. Originally they must have been placed on the bottom boards of the ship, or possibly on a low-lying, specially constructed floor, perhaps at the level of the fourth strake (*70*). The centre of interest, to those laying out the funeral deposit, had been the west, or after end of the chamber, where ceremonial objects and the jewelled trappings and weapons of the dead man lay. Kitchen utensils and more ordinary objects were at the east, or forward, end of the chamber. The dead man had been visualized as lying facing the bow of his vessel, the direction in which it would travel. His helmet lay to the west, as did the sword pommel, while the shoes were placed beneath the great dish to the east. No body was found, however, and it is not certain that any was ever present (p. 69). The grave goods had been crushed and disturbed in varying degrees by the collapse of the burial chamber, when many tons of overburden fell on the deposit.

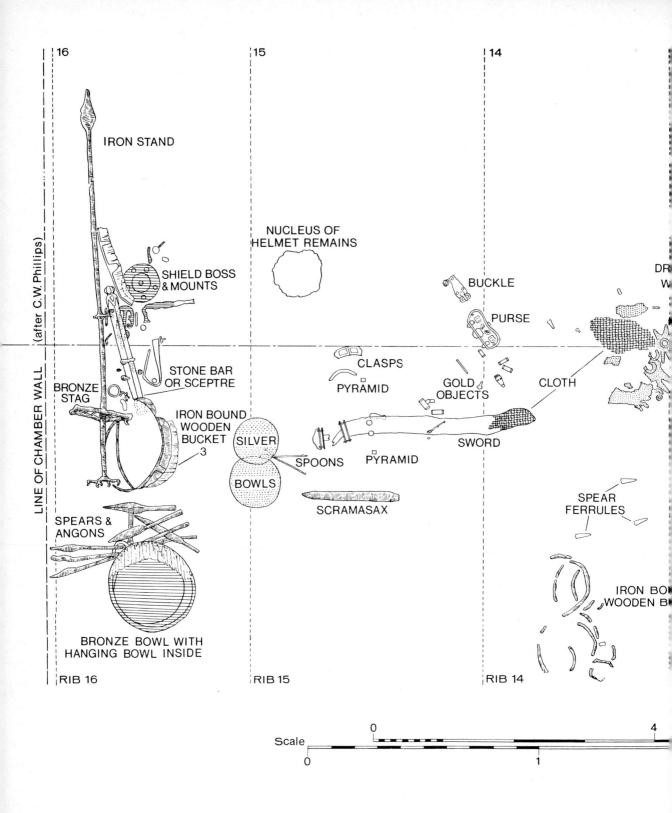

16

15

14

IRON STAND

(after C.W. Phillips)

NUCLEUS OF
HELMET REMAINS

BUCKLE

PURSE

SHIELD BOSS
& MOUNTS

CLASPS

PYRAMID

GOLD
OBJECTS

CLOTH

LINE OF CHAMBER WALL

STONE BAR
OR SCEPTRE

BRONZE
STAG

IRON BOUND
WOODEN
BUCKET

SILVER

SWORD

3

SPOONS

PYRAMID

BOWLS

SCRAMASAX

SPEAR
FERRULES

SPEARS &
ANGONS

IRON BO
WOODEN B

BRONZE BOWL WITH
HANGING BOWL INSIDE

RIB 16

RIB 15

RIB 14

DR
W

Scale

0

0

1

4

7   *Plan of the burial-deposit.*

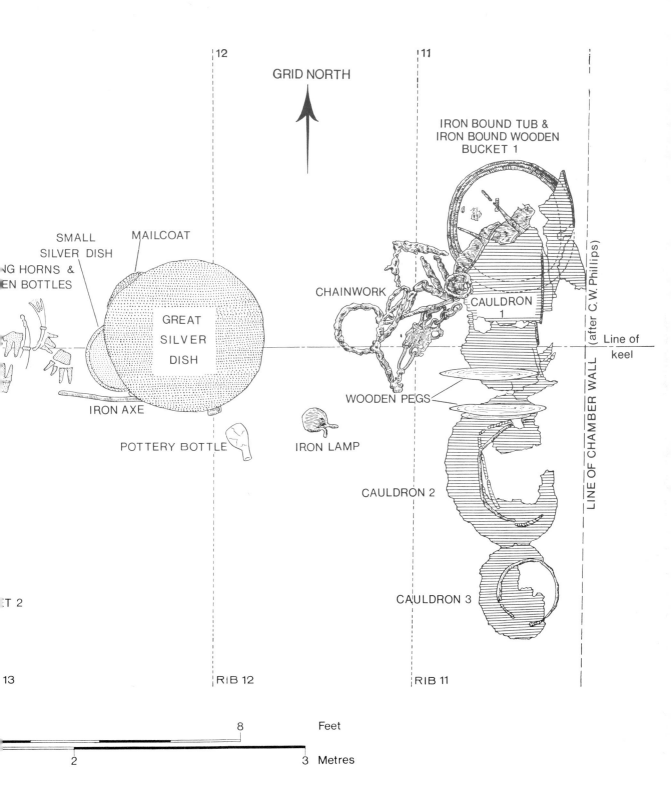

GRID NORTH

12

11

IRON BOUND TUB &
IRON BOUND WOODEN
BUCKET 1

SMALL
SILVER DISH

MAILCOAT

NG HORNS &
EN BOTTLES

CHAINWORK

CAULDRON
1

GREAT
SILVER
DISH

Line of
keel

LINE OF CHAMBER WALL (after C.W. Phillips)

IRON AXE

WOODEN PEGS

POTTERY BOTTLE

IRON LAMP

CAULDRON 2

T 2

CAULDRON 3

13

RIB 12

RIB 11

8   Feet

2   3   Metres

OBJECTS DEPOSITED ACROSS
THE WEST END OF THE BURIAL CHAMBER

The Iron Stand

Lying along the west wall of the chamber was a remarkable iron object, at first thought to be perhaps a portable beacon or flambeau. It may be something of this kind. On the other hand it may, as is discussed below, be a kind of standard (*8*). It is 5 ft 6 in. (165 cm) high, with a short spike and two volutes or treads at the bottom. At the top is a horizontally-set iron plate with four short projecting arms, each terminating in a simplified inward-facing ox-head executed in wrought iron. Eleven inches lower down the shaft passed through the centre of a large rectangular iron grille, the four corners of which were also ornamented with ox-heads. The corners of this grille are connected with another much smaller iron plate or fitting lower down by four converging twisted iron rods, which give a cage-like structure. This whole object was badly rusted and bent, and is in very fragile condition. A modern reconstruction is exhibited near the original.

The point below the volutes or 'treads' at the lower end of the stand is short, only some 4½ in. (11.5 cm) in length, and the superstructure seems too heavy to have been held up securely by so small a point without other support if, when in use, it was further loaded with branches, pennants, or anything which might explain its odd construction. This suggests the possibility that the point may have been intended not to stick in the ground but rather to engage in a leather holster or frog, so that the whole object could be supported and carried by a strap over the shoulders,[6] after the fashion of modern regimental colours. On the other hand, the new reconstruction made in 1971 is appreciably lighter than the old, and can certainly support itself in firm and favourable soil.

'Standards' (*segn*) in the Old English epic poem *Beowulf* (see p. 82 below) are associated with ships and with buried treasure, and Beowulf himself was presented with one, described as gilded, and evidently of metal, as part of his reward for the slaying of Grendel.[7] Standards are usually referred to in the literary sources as 'golden' or 'gold adorned'.[8] The Sutton Hoo 'standard', neither golden nor gilt, but of wrought iron, and a portable object, comparable in size and weight to the Roman legionary *signum*, may possibly, especially if filled with foliage, peacock feathers or the like, be the special type of standard called by the Romans *tufa*, and by the English *thuuf* (a tuft of feathers) which according to the great English historian, the Venerable Bede, who died in AD 735, Edwin, King of Northumbria, the Saxon Bretwalda, or High King (*d.* 632) was accustomed to have borne before him on his royal progresses, wherever he went, in the Roman manner.[9] Edwin might well have learnt this ceremonial during the period of exile which he spent at the East

Anglian court, perhaps at Rendlesham (*1*),[10] with Raedwald (p. 95) whom he succeeded as Bretwalda. Since the coin evidence (ch. VI) allows the possibility that the Sutton Hoo burial is Raedwald's the iron stand might well be a *tufa* carried before him to mark his status as High King.

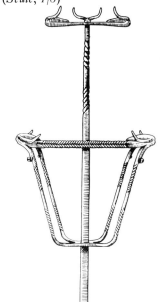

8 *The iron stand, restored.* (*Scale, 1/8*)

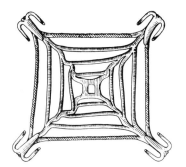

The Sceptre (3, 9–13)

Alongside the iron stand was a remarkable four-sided symmetrically designed stone bar, 2 ft (61 cm) in length and weighing 6 lb 4 oz (*9*). It tapers evenly towards the ends, each of which terminates in a roughly spherical knob. One of these is squat and slightly flattened. Both are painted red and both have a central outward projection, on the axis of the stone, of truncated conical form. One knob is surmounted by a small bronze saucer fixed to the stone bar by a cage of light bronze ribs. These spring from the deep base-ring of the saucer, which fits over the projection on the stone, and their lower ends are held in by a bronze ring or collar round the constriction below the knob. The bronze terminal of the other end was missing. A sombre human face in a pear-shaped frame is carved on each face of the stone below the knobs at either end. At one end (that to which the saucer is attached) three out of four faces are bearded, and two are moustached (*10*): on the five other heads long hair appears below the chin, but in all instances except one it is depicted as though growing out of the neck and as not connected with the hair of the head. If this treatment of the hair under the chin, which is done with deliberation and stands in sharp contrast to the rendering of beards in the manifestly bearded heads, is not intended to depict an off-the-chin beard, then these faces, which are also smaller and more delicately featured, are perhaps intended to represent women.

Right and opposite:
9–11 *The stone sceptre,
overall view and details.
(Scale, overall view, 1/4)*

The stone is beautifully shaped and in mint condition. It is of very fine grain, and of the general type of stone used for whetstones in this period and later. However, it shows no sign of having ever been used for sharpening. The sharp angles between the four sides show only a slight polish, presumably from handling. The object is too large and heavy to be carried for any practical purpose on the person. There is indeed no reason to speak of it as a whetstone. It is a stone bar, of long and narrow form, and fine grain, and here the analogy ends. It has always been thought that this impressive and unique object must have had some ceremonial import, and this has been put beyond reasonable doubt by recent developments in the study of the stone bar and of the iron stand just described. For some twenty-five years, students and visitors have been accustomed to seeing mounted on top of the iron stand a bronze stag (*3*, *12*) on a vertically set iron ring, the ends of which in turn are fixed into Y-shaped arms spreading out from a bronze pedestal. It has become clear that there is not only no evidence of any kind that this stag on its bronze pedestal ever stood on the top of the iron stand, but strong negative evidence against its having done so. On the other hand there are good reasons for regarding the stag, ring and pedestal as the missing terminal from the stone bar. The evidence for this association is set out in full in the Museum's definitive publication. Suffice it here

12 *Bronze stag mounted on an iron wire ring fitted into a bronze pedestal. From the sceptre, see 13. (Scale, 4/5)*

to say that it is at once formal, circumstantial and metallurgical. With this enhancement it becomes less possible to think of the object as in any way functional, inevitable that it should be regarded as a ceremonial piece; and in this evidently secular context it is difficult to interpret it as anything other than a royal sceptre (*13*).

The fine-grained stone may have been chosen for its suitability for handling and for delicate small-scale carving, and stone as such for some latent power or significance deemed to reside in the substance itself. If it were also conceived as representing a whetstone it would symbolize in a striking way, as Sir Thomas Kendrick once suggested, the Saxon king in the role of Wayland the Smith—the forger, giver and master of the swords of his following. It is, at all events, an impressive object which has already claimed the serious attention of historians concerned to establish its place amongst the emblems and instruments of royal power. Such an explanation does not preclude the possibility that the stone also had magical or religious properties. Germanic kings sought to trace their descent from their gods, in the case of the Wuffingas, from Woden.

In trying to assess the meaning of the stone, we must seek to answer several questions. Why is the object made of stone? What is the significance of the bronze saucer? Why are the knobs painted red (the colour of blood)? What is the meaning of the eight faces? Any answers which we can offer must be speculative, but there can be little doubt that this great ceremonial stone is an object of magic and potency, whether in enlisting the aid of ancestors or warding off evil. With no redeeming sign of Christianity added to it, it seems to reflect essentially a pagan outlook. Two German scholars sum up their estimate of it as follows:

Our view is that those especial powers and influences that established the fortunes of the Sutton Hoo royal house were incapsulated in this staff, as Odin's divine strength was in his spear.[11]

At this time they were unaware of the added factor of the stag as the missing terminal. What is its significance?

Several less monumental and less delicately shaped stones of fine grain exist which might be regarded as whetstones and which terminate in carved heads at least at one end (in each case only one end survives). They are all probably of this period. Three are from the Celtic north and west, and one from an Anglo-Saxon grave at Hough-on-the-Hill, Lincolnshire. One, from Lochar Moss in Dumfrieshire, is of substantial proportions; that from Hough-on-the-Hill is also of large size, though the representation of the head is crude.[12] But nothing at all is known that begins to approach in complexity, sophistication, quality, awesomeness or finish this fantastic piece from Sutton Hoo.

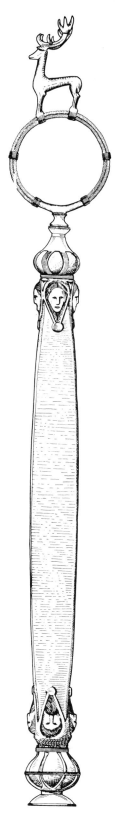

13 *The sceptre. (Scale, 1/4)*

31

The Shield (*14–16, 19–23*)

To the north of the ceremonial stone were the remains of a large circular shield (*7, 15*). These comprised a large and heavy ornamented iron boss with five large domed gilt-bronze rivet-heads on the flange and a disc at the apex (*16*); and metal mounts and fittings mostly in the form of, or decorated with, stylized animals and bird or animal heads (*20–23*). The rotted wood of the shield survived here and there in patches of wafer-thinness. The heavy boss, taking its attached metal fittings with it, had sunk through the rotten wood to a lower level, and the wooden frame had later been pushed into a more or less rectangular shape by the bulging in of the chamber's end-wall (*7*). The remains of the shield board, which were not at the time seen in relation to the shield-boss, were at first taken for the remains of a wooden tray. The flange of the shield-boss was covered with panels of gilt-bronze sheeting carrying an embossed design of two stylized pairs of confronted horses, rearing up on their hind legs (*21, 84c*).

The diameter of the shield has been calculated as about 36 in.[13] The shield was not flat, but curved. The shield-board was covered front and back with leather, and on this the various fittings rested. Whether this leather was stained or painted is not known. Amongst mounts or fittings from the front of the shield are the head and leg of a bird of prey in gilt-bronze and remains of its body in patterned gold foil in very poor condition. The projecting crest at the back of the bird's head is in the form of another bird or dragon head, and a simplified human face appears in the garnet inlay in a pear-shaped field on the bird's hip (*20*). This face, with its sharply pointed frame, 'stopped' at the point by an orange inlay, has affinities with the bearded faces on the sceptre (*10*). The bird's head and leg are of cast bronze. A second mount is a dragon-like creature with fierce teeth and three pairs of wings and terminating pair of feet. In addition to the bird and dragon there were four small gilt bosses of the same size as those on the flange of the shield-boss (*16*) and fragments of patterned gold foil representing other decorative features including a long strip tapering to either end.[14] Some of this gold foil represents additional decorative features associated with the rim.

14   *Gilt bronze 'ring' similar to rings found on the hilts of ring-swords, mounted on the lower half of the shield, see 19. (Scale, 1/1)*

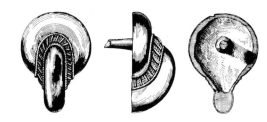

A solitary 'ring' (*14*) was subsequently found in the Museum laboratory in a lump of sand associated with fragments of the shield. It is of gilt-bronze, not of gold. Although it resembles the fitting of a 'ring-sword', the use of inferior material and the lack of space on the gold sword pommel showed that the ring certainly did not come from the sword in the burial. The recent discovery of a matching alderwood and leather underlay finally proved that the ring had been mounted on the shield-board. It is an object of symbolic significance.[15] A similarly shaped 'sword-ring' has been found in a Swedish boat-grave mounted on a drinking-horn.[16] It will be noted that the lobe of the ring that would stand vertically when the ring was mounted is not cut away obliquely to fit onto the side of a pommel, as it invariably is in the developed sword-rings. The ring appears to be yet another Swedish element in the grave. It shares its uncut vertical lobe and lack of connection with a sword, uniquely with the ring from the contemporary Swedish boat-grave, and the narrow oblong section of its vertical lobe, the flattened shape of the horizontal ring, and the decorative filigree band sealing the junction between the two, occur again amongst known sword-rings only in the added ring of a well-known sword-hilt of about AD 600 from Vallstenarum, Gotland, in the Statens Historiska Museum, Stockholm.[17]

15 *The shield-boss and mounts and fittings of the shield as uncovered in the ground.*

The iron grip at the back of the shield-boss is deliberately placed off-centre, to the right. This allows the knuckles and the back of the left hand to fit into the cavity inside the boss. The grip is extended at either end by a gilt-bronze ornamental strip, which terminates in an animal head with garnet eyes (*23*). The curved arms which spring out from these grip extensions to either side terminate in bird- and dragon-heads, also with garnet eyes. Near one end of the grip-extension on the back of the shield lay a silver-plated bronze fitting with a central loop, to which a silvered strap-end is attached by a ring. This strap-end may have terminated a leather strap by which the shield was carried or hung up when not in use. The other end of the strap was found in position attached to the upper end of the grip.

Opposite: 17
The helmet. New reconstruction, 1971.

16   *The shield-boss. (Scale, about 3/4)*

The fittings from the sword including the pommel, guard-plates, circular scabbard bosses, pyramidal mounts from the suspension-strap or sword-knot and two filigree clips from the grip. (Scale, approximately 3/2)

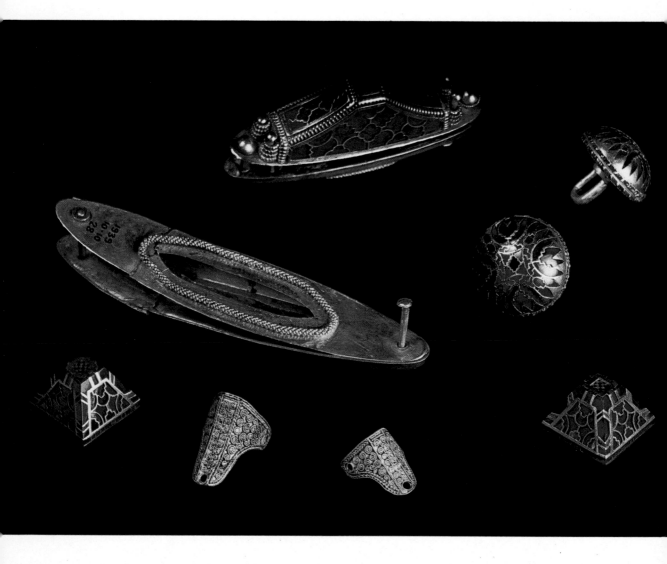

The shield is remarkably similar in certain respects to those found in the earliest of the boat-graves in the Swedish cemetery at Vendel.[18] The gnashing teeth of the dragon and of the animal snouts on the Sutton Hoo shield (22, 23) recur frequently in the Vendel material. Human faces very like that on the bird's hip on the Sutton Hoo shield are set in the interlace on the flange of the shield-boss from Vendel, grave XII, a burial which is dated by Swedish archaeologists to about AD 650.

19   *The reconstructed shield.*

20 *Gilt-bronze bird from the front of the shield. (Scale, 1/2)*

21 *Design of inter-linked horses stamped in gilt-bronze foil, from the flange of the shield-boss. (Scale, 1/1)*

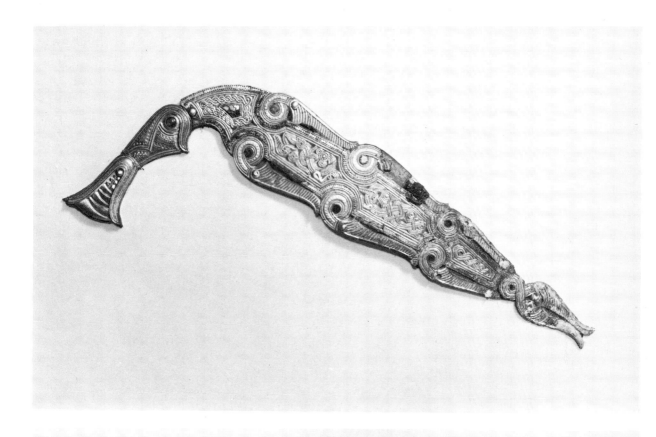

Bucket No. III

By the head of the standard at its south end were the remains of an iron-bound wooden bucket, fourteen inches (35 cm) in diameter, and about the same in height. This was no doubt placed in this dignified context for the sake of its contents, perhaps wine or mead, or a favourite food.

Top: **22** *Gilt-bronze winged dragon, part of the fittings from the front of the shield.* (*Scale, 1/2*)

23 *Ornamental grip-extension in gilt-bronze from the back of the shield.* (*Scale, 2/3*)

Heavy Bronze Bowl, Hanging-Bowl, Musical Instrument and Spear Complex (24)

To the south of the standard and the bucket was a substantial bronze bowl with drop handles and a base ring. On the inside of the bowl, in the field between a plain central roundel and an outer zone of shallow peripheral flutings, are naturalistic outline engravings of a camel, a donkey, a lion and another large feline in procession (25). The bowl is not of local manufacture and must have come from the Near East, probably Alexandria. It is of a type known in the archaeology of the period as 'Coptic bowls', i.e. from Christian, or Coptic, Egypt.[19] Inside the bronze bowl were found the remains of a large hanging-bowl of thin bronze, of Celtic workmanship, a type of vessel not infrequently found in Anglo-Saxon graves (26). It has eight well-preserved enamelled decorative escutcheons, three of which, of circular form, are cast in one piece with hooks for suspension of the bowl (4, 28), hooks which terminate, on the rim of the bowl, in what are apparently intended to represent

24 *Heavy bronze 'Coptic' bowl with drop handles, large bronze hanging-bowl (inside the Coptic bowl) and complex of spears, as uncovered by the excavators.*

seals' heads. The centre escutcheon on the bottom of the bowl inside supports a little pedestal on which, lying horizontally $1\frac{1}{2}$ in. (3.8 cm) high in the interior of the bowl, is a bronze fish, cast in the round and originally spotted with sunken studs of enamel (*27*). It can be rotated with the finger. The bowl had worn through or sustained damage before it was buried, and had been patched in several places with riveted silver plates. The largest of these patches (*29*) is decorated at each end on the face that showed inside the bowl with birds' heads. These birds' heads are similar to those on the purse, the great buckle and the metal fittings associated with the musical instrument to be described shortly (*30, 31*).

25 *Procession of animals in shallow engraving on the inside of the Coptic bowl,* see 24. *(Scale, approximately 1/4)*

Of the enamelled escutcheons fixed to the upper part of the bowl, three are circular and three are square. Beneath each of the circular escutcheons is a cast bronze fitting of triangular shape, in the form of an animal head (*4*). The sunken eyes were filled with circular garnets, backed by patterned gold foil discs. The bowl had been repaired by a Germanic goldsmith, as the silver patch with 'Style II' birds' heads shows, and the foil and garnet fillings of the eyes in the animal heads must be a secondary feature, substituted by the Saxon goldsmith for lost original fillings of enamel. This hanging-bowl, though damaged, ranks as the most richly ornamented and important of some seventy examples of the fifth–seventh-century period at present known.[20] A notable feature of its embellishment is the use of *millefiori* glass insets, and also of translucent glass. The *millefiori* insets, of which the bowl shows a wide range, are mostly of minute intricate chess-board or rosette-like patterns, and are individually planted in the general red enamel field. The patterns are composed at a very much larger scale in bundles of coloured glass rods of varying cross-sections, and the pattern is then reduced by heating the bundle of rods until soft and drawing it out like chewing-gum, perhaps for 30 or 40 feet, so greatly reducing the cross-section.

26 *General view of the large hanging-bowl. (Scale, about 1/3)*

27 *The fish on a pedestal from the interior of the large hanging-bowl—the fins and tail are damaged. (Scale, 1/1)*

When cool, the resultant glass cord is cut in small sections which are inlaid cold into the enamel field on the object to be decorated. The *millefiori*, set within a curvilinear pattern executed in abnormal translucent blue glass used in a manner not paralleled on any other hanging-bowl, can be well seen on the basal escutcheon. Around the central roundel that contains this design is an exquisite Celtic hair-line pattern of running scrolls reserved in bronze against the red enamel ground, and executed with the greatest delicacy.

28   *Detail of a rectangular escutcheon from the large hanging-bowl. (Scale, 2/1)*

29   *Silver patch from the large hanging-bowl. (Scale, 1/1)*

43

The Lyre

Inside the hanging-bowl were remains of a small six-stringed musical instrument with wooden pegs. It was of maplewood, with pegs of poplar or willow, and was apparently kept and buried in a beaver-skin bag, with the fur inside. Beaver hairs were found adhering all over the outer surfaces of the wood. The frame of the instrument was ornamented with two square gilt-bronze plaques with projecting birds' heads. These were countersunk into the frame, and were functional, holding pairs of rivets which held fast tenon and mortice joints. The instrument was reconstructed in 1948 as a small harp of rectangular outline some 15 in. (37.5 cm) high, but the subsequent discovery of a large number of extra fragments of maplewood and associated oak called for a reconsideration of its shape and features, which has led finally to its reconstruction as a symmetrical instrument some 29 inches in length—a Germanic 'round lyre'. For the new reconstruction, which called for much skilful and prolonged work in the assembly and analysis of wood fragments, and of other complex evidence, I am indebted to Miss Myrtle Bruce-Mitford, Mrs V. Fenwick, and Mrs G. Keiller. A replica of the lyre was made in the workshops of Arnold Dolmetsch Ltd, from working drawings supplied by the Museum (*31*).

The surviving original fragments of maplewood, with the pegs and the metal escutcheons, are illustrated (*30*). Note the cut-out area in the arm on the left of the picture. Hollow arms, serving as an extension of the resonating space, are a feature of all the known lyre-remains of this period. The arms and soundbox were fashioned from a single piece of wood, and a thin wooden lid covered the hollowed area. In the case of the Sutton Hoo lyre, the lid was held in position by headless pins of bronze. The soundbox proper did not survive, since this portion of the instrument fell outside the hanging-bowl and was destroyed by the acid sandy soil; its length in the reconstruction is based mainly on the evidence of remains of contemporary lyres from German graves at Oberflacht, Württemburg[21] and St Severin's Church, Cologne.

The bridge and the tailpiece had likewise disappeared. The bridge used in the replica is a copy in bone of an eighth century amber one from Broa i Halle in Gotland. If the Sutton Hoo bridge had been of amber—a stable substance—traces would probably have survived. The existence of a bone bridge of a slightly later date, from Birka, in Sweden, justified the use of bone in this case. In the absence of any positive evidence for the shape of the tailpiece the lyre has been equipped with a purely functional one of the simplest design.[22] The small knob at the bottom, to which the tailpiece is fastened, is a feature of two of the German lyres already mentioned.

The model has been strung with gut, though other materials are possible. Nothing is known about the tuning of stringed instruments

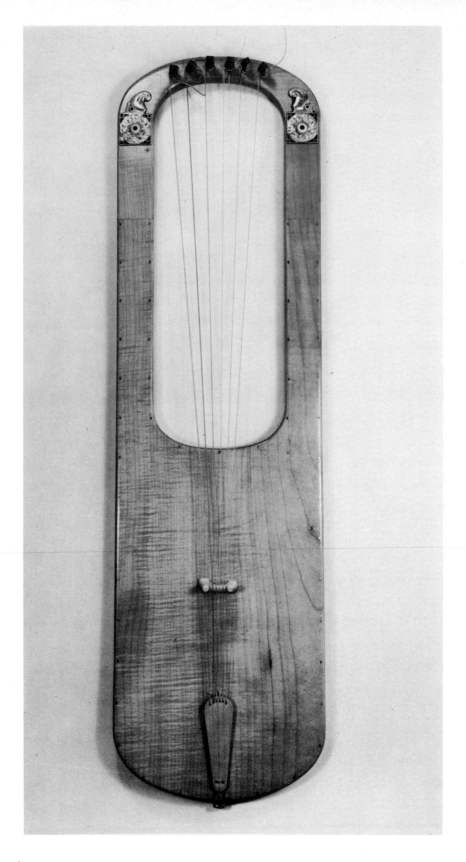

of this period; a pentatonic scale as used in early folk music is a possibility, but other methods have been suggested. The instrument has no sound-holes, but is nevertheless surprisingly resonant. The pitch is somewhere between the alto and tenor registers.

Spears and Angons

Through one of the drop-handles of the large bronze bowl were thrust three long iron throwing spears of the type known as *angons* (*24*). With them lay five socketed iron spear-heads. Further east lay another large spear blade (formerly identified as a scramasax or knife). The ferrules from the shafts of the angons were later found about 7 ft to the east. All these iron objects were much broken and very badly corroded.

Silver Bowls and Spoons

Three feet out from the west wall a dome-like lump, with purplish stains, proved to be a nest of eight inverted silver bowls, one inside the other, and all except the top two perfectly preserved (*32*, *77*). Two more bowls, similar to the others, had slid off the top of the pile. One of these had almost completely disintegrated. Under the silver bowls, their handles projecting, were two silver spoons of Byzantine type, inlaid in niello (a black paste, consisting at this period only of silver sulphide[23]) with the names 'Saulos' and 'Paulos' (Saul and Paul) in Greek characters (*33*, *78*). These and other silver pieces from the grave are more fully described in Chapter VIII.

32 *Two of a set of ten shallow silver bowls. (Scale, 1/3)*

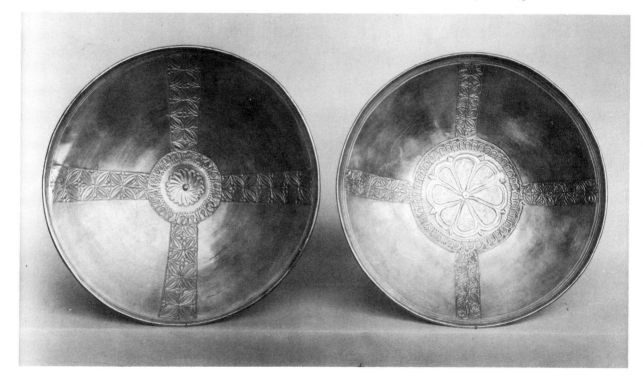

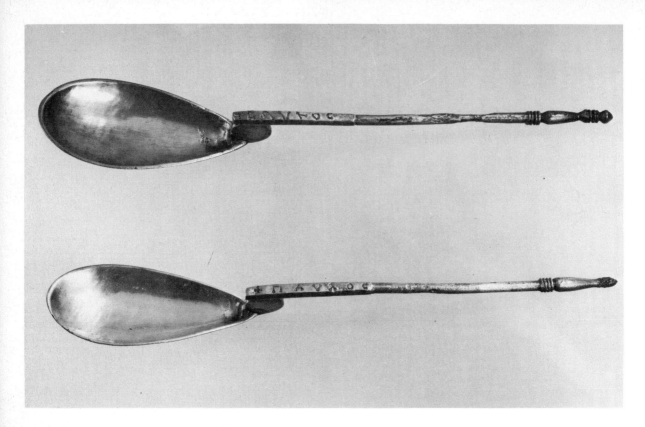

33 *Pair of silver spoons with the names Saul and Paul in Greek. (Scale, approximately 3/5)*

The Helmet[24]

On the north side of the keel-line and about 3 or 4 ft out from the west wall of the chamber were many small corroded and fragile fragments of a shattered iron helmet, closely similar to those found in Swedish boatgraves at Vendel and Valsgärde. It had a D-shaped iron crest inlaid with silver wires in chevron pattern, and bronze eyebrows inlaid with silver wires in close-set vertical lines. Each eyebrow terminates in a small gilt-bronze boar's head, and the under-edge of each brow is picked out with a line of small, square-cut garnets, set in metal cells. Other features are an iron visor carrying a gilt-bronze nose, mouth and upper lip, the nose in full relief and the upper lip furnished with a close-trimmed moustache; hinged iron cheek-pieces and an iron neck-guard thrust out at an angle (*17, 34*). The iron crown, as in the Swedish helmets mentioned above, was originally covered with thin bronze plates, parts of which survive. In the Sutton Hoo helmet these plates were tinned. Narrow ribs of fluted metal were riveted over these, concealing the junctions between the plates and dividing the crown up into panels. The panels in the lowest row, running around the base of the crown like a hatband, were embossed with at least two figural designs in semi-naturalistic style. The two that can be reconstructed depict armed warriors in a battle scene and twin dancing figures (*36*). Only small fragments survive, but each of the two scenes is repeated a number of

Opposite:
34 *The Sutton Hoo helmet replica made in the Tower of London Armouries.*

35 *Composite reconstruction of one of the three figural scenes that decorated the helmet. The scene was repeated six times on the helmet, and is here built up from different fragments surviving from the various impressions. A rider on horseback with big head and small shield, brandishing a spear, is shown riding down a fallen warrior. (Scale 2/1)*

36 *Reconstruction of the scene of dancing warriors from the Sutton Hoo helmet. (Scale, 2/1)*

times. The largest surviving fragment of a second subject may be seen above the helmet's right eyebrow. Reconstructions of the whole of these scenes are given in *35, 36*. A few fragments of a third figural scene have also been identified. The first scene occurs also in a vertical sequence in the middle of each side of the helmet, the topmost occurrence abutting on the crest. The twin warrior scene also appears once on each cheek-piece.

Panels elsewhere on the crown and on the visor and cheek- and neck-guards are decorated with interlace ornament in a variety of the style known to archaeologists as Style II, and related to interlace on the Swedish shield-bosses and other pieces from Vendel, graves XI and XII.

As restored, the helmet has the outsize dimensions of a crash-helmet, which implies, as might be expected, the presence of padding or shock-absorbing material of some kind between the iron crown and the wearer's head. Leather seems to have formed at least part of this protective inner lining. A silver inlaid iron crest runs from back to front over the cap; the fluted bronze strips which flank its length were gilded. The crest terminates at either end in a gilt-bronze animal head with long gnashing teeth and garnet eyes. Its middle portion is well preserved, and there is nothing about it to suggest that the helmet was originally crowned with the figure of a boar or a bird, like helmets described in the literature of the era, and illustrated on the figured panels of some of the Swedish helmets mentioned above. Even without this crowning feature, however, the silver and gold helmet, enhanced by the glitter of its gems, with living eyes behind its mask, must have been an awe-inspiring spectacle (*17*). It is a most dramatic object, different in important respects from all the similar Swedish-found helmets and unique in this country.

The new reconstruction of the helmet illustrated (*17*), is as completed in 1971, the work of Mr Nigel Williams, then a Conservation Officer in the Department of Medieval and Later Antiquities. The new reconstruction differs in many respects from the old. A very striking feature is the incorporation (at the back of the crest) of a third dragon head, not accounted for in the old reconstruction. This has made possible a rearrangement of the other two heads in which one is placed pointing upwards on top of the gilt-bronze nose-piece and may be seen as forming a bird-like figure, with the eyebrows as wings and the moustache as a fanned tail. This should probably be regarded as a flying dragon (like that with three pairs of wings on the shield, *22*) rather than a bird. It encounters the snake-like dragon represented by the crest and its zoomorphic terminals head on.

The cheek-pieces, presumably tied under the chin by tapes sewn to the lining, can fit closely, when so tied, against the new profile of the face-mask. The neck-guard is broad and the protection afforded is complete and uninterrupted around the circuit of the head.

OBJECTS DEPOSITED ALONG THE KEEL-LINE

The Sword and the Gold Jewellery

To the east of the objects so far described, down the centre of the burial-chamber along the keel-line, was an amazing series of gold objects jewelled with garnets and *millefiori* glass. They were spread over an area about 3 ft by 3 ft 6 in. With them lay a rusted sword (*37*) with jewelled gold pommel and hilt (*18*). Prominent amongst this series of magnificent

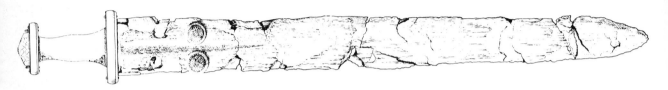

37   The sword with jewelled gold pommel and hilt. (Scale, 1/5)

jewels as they lay in the ground was a great gold buckle (*79*), a pair of heavy curved clasps hinging centrally about long gold pins (*39, 73*), and a purse-lid, consisting of a jewelled gold frame containing seven ornamental plaques and four circular enamelled studs (*80*). On the purse-lid, which was found lying upside down in the ground, were thirty-seven gold coins, three circular blank flans of coin size, and two small gold ingots (*38, 75*). These and some thirteen other gold jewels (*40, 41*) lay haphazard in the sand, apparently in no intelligible arrangement, some face downwards, and at all angles (*38*). The torque which the scatter of strap-mounts exhibited suggested to the excavators that they had originally been fixed to a leather harness suspended from the roof of the burial chamber, which had fallen either with the collapse of the chamber, or earlier. The gold jewellery and the sword are described more fully in Chapter IX.

Drinking-horns and drinking-vessels

To the east of the sword and gold jewellery, still on the keel-line, was an area containing the crushed and disintegrated remains of a group of outstanding drinking-vessels, such as would grace a royal hall or table. They had been covered with cloth, remains of which survived. Two of the vessels were drinking-horns of unusual size, made from the horns of the now extinct aurochs. The restoration formerly published has been shown to be incorrect. New reconstructions of smaller mouth-diameter and capacity but the same length have been made (*42*). The remaining vessels, six in number, were of maplewood and were 6–7 in. (15–17.5

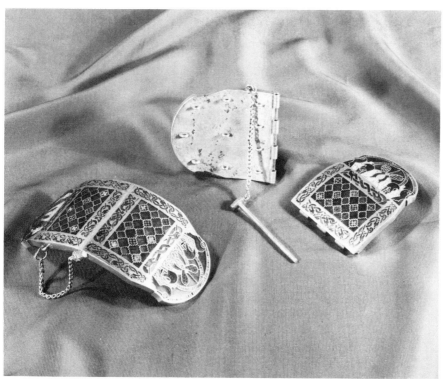

38 *The purse-lid (seen upside-down), the great gold buckle and subsidiary buckles and mounts, as uncovered in the ground.*

39 *Pair of hinged shoulder-clasps. (Scale, 1/2)* See also 73.

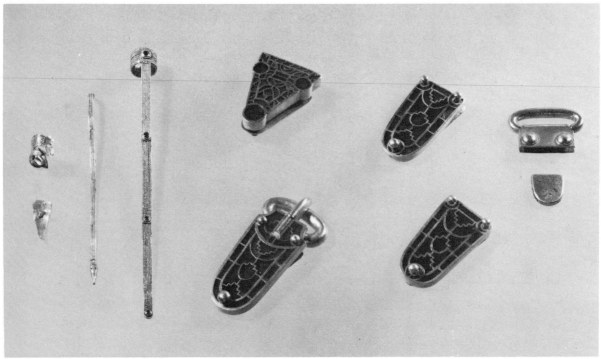

cm) in height. They were apparently of globular form and had cylindrical necks. The shape of their lower part cannot be established, but a likely reconstruction is suggested in *44* and *72*. The vessels had identical mounts and must have formed a set of approximately the same size and shape. Both the drinking-horns and the wooden vessels were decorated around their mouths with rectangular silver-gilt panels and immediately below these with a series of long triangular mounts, or vandykes, pendant on the drinking-horns, radiating on the globular vessels.[25] Panels and triangles were stamped with designs of animal ornament. One die had been used for all the rectangular panels on the horns, and a second for all the triangular mounts. This is also the case with the maplewood vessels, but here different and smaller dies were used. The two sets of designs are shown in *43* and *45*. It seems that the two great horns were a pair, and the maplewood vessels a set. The solid tips of the great horns were elaborately encased in silver-gilt (*42*). Each had a finial ending in a bird's head, and was decorated with panels of cast animal ornament, cloisonné-pattern inlays in niello, cast collars and panels of stamped foil showing interlace and animal ornament. The restorations of the bottles are by Mr Nigel Williams.

One parallel for these maplewood bottles exists, not previously recognized.[26] Wooden cups, however, with silver-gilt mounts are not uncommon in rich Anglo-Saxon graves.[27]

The fact that the great drinking-horns, which dwarf the smaller maplewood bottles, are made from the horns of an aurochs gives them a peculiar interest. *Ūruz* (aurochs) in Old English, in Germanic, *Ur*, is the name given to one of the symbols of the runic 'alphabet', the series of angular characters developed as a form or writing, imbued with magic and mystery, amongst the early Germanic peoples. To quote a recent work 'ritual, religion, magic, symbolic associations, cling to most of the names given to the runic symbols'.[28] The name *Ūruz* suggests the concept of manly strength 'for hunting and slaying of the aurochs was almost a ritual amongst the Germanic tribes and great fame derived from it'. Caesar (*De Bello Gallico*, vi, 28) is our authority for this, and the passage is worth quoting in full. Writing of rare animals, he says this:

A third species is that which they call aurochs. These are somewhat smaller in size, than elephants, and are like bulls in appearance, colour and shape. Great is their strength and great is their speed, and once they have spied man or beast they do not spare them. These the Germani capture skilfully in pits; and their young men harden themselves by such labour and exercise themselves by this kind of hunting. And those who have slain most of the beasts bring the horns as evidence thereof to a public place and win great fame. The animals, even if caught very young, cannot be tamed or accustomed to human beings. Their horns differ very much from those of our oxen in size and shape, and kind. The Germani collect them eagerly, encase their edges in silver, and use them as beakers at their most magnificent banquets.

Opposite top:
40 *Rectangular mounts, buckle and strap-distributor, and a curved buckle with dummy tongue, from the royal harness. (Scale, about 1/2)*
Opposite bottom:
41 *Smaller strap-ends, buckles and miscellaneous fittings. The use of the fittings on the left are uncertain. The small curled-up animal (top left) and the strip with ring-head were apparently mounted on the same object. (Scale, about 3/4)*

55

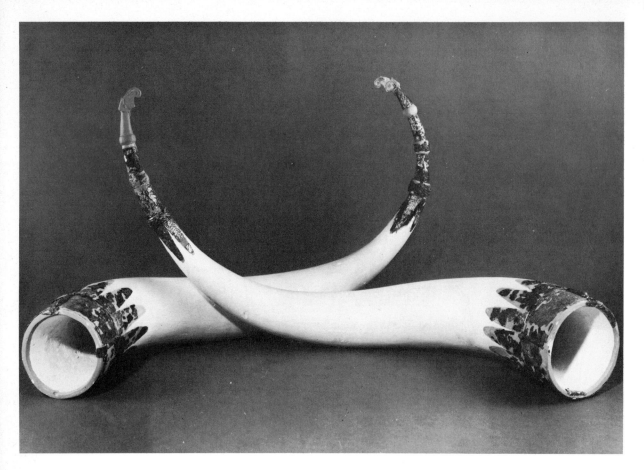

42 *The great drinking horns.*
(Scale, 1/4)

43 *Animal-ornament designs of silver-gilt mounts from the aurochs' horns. (a) rectangular panel repeated six times to form the horizontal zone of ornament below the rim. Flanking the panel are two of the cast clips, with double human masks, which held the panels in position; (b) triangular mount or 'van-dyke', one of twenty-one surrounding the horn below the horizontal panels.*
(Scale, 1/1)

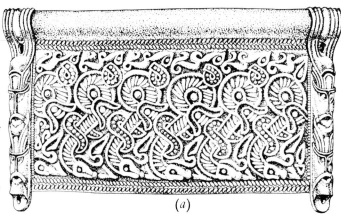

(a)

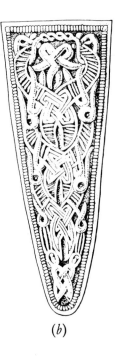

(b)

The two great aurochs' horns at Sutton Hoo were both mounted round the rim with silver-gilt mounts (*43a*) and their terminals with silver-gilt foil patterns and with bird's head finials (*42*), all work of very high quality. Here in the Sutton Hoo burial are preserved the very mementoes of manly valour that Caesar is describing. The tradition had survived for seven centuries from Caesar's day.

The aurochs' horn-cores on which the former giant reconstructions, seven inches in diameter at the mouth and with a capacity of six quarts, were based, were those of an inter-glacial breed known now to have become extinct by the time of Tacitus, having suffered the process of post-Pleistocene dwarfing. The creature hunted in Tacitus' day, if much smaller, was still, as his account suggests, a very large and formidable animal.

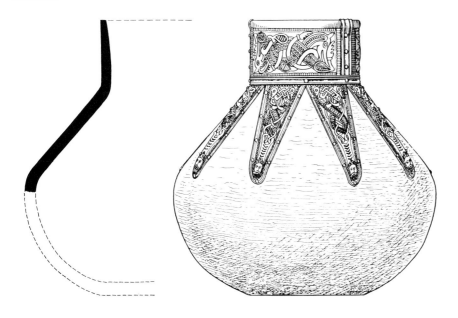

44 *Reconstruction drawing of one of the maplewood bottles. (Scale, 1/2)*

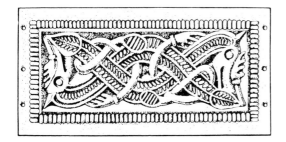

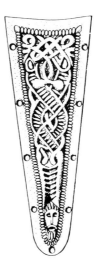

45 *Animal-ornament designs of silver-gilt mounts from the maplewood bottles. (Scale, 1/1)*

The Great Silver Dish and Objects under it

To the east of the drinking-horns was a great circular object which proved to be a huge silver dish (*46, 49–51*). It was 28½ in. (73 cm) in diameter, and bore, under the base, control stamps, in two varieties, of the Byzantine Emperor Anastasius I (AD 491–518) (*50, 51*), showing that it was made within the frontiers of the Byzantine Empire, and probably assayed in Constantinople itself, between those years. From beneath the great dish an iron bar and part of a smaller silver dish could be seen projecting (*52*). When the great dish was lifted, the iron bar was found to be the handle of an axe-hammer (*47*), probably a tool rather than a weapon. The whole overall length was about 2 ft 6 in. (76.5 cm). The handle ended in a small ring, and through this a larger ring had been forged. The smaller silver dish was a sizeable fluted bowl with two drop-handles.[29] In the centre of the bowl, in a circular field, was a woman's head in relief in classical style, in profile and with hair gathered back into a 'bun' (*53, 82*).

Under the great silver dish there was also a mass of partly decomposed cloth and leather and flock-like material identified by ornithologists in the British Museum (Natural History) as goose down, probably the stuffing of a pillow. There was also a silver cup, 3½ in. (9 cm) in diameter, with a foot ring (*54*), and inside the fluted bowl a small silver ladle, ornamented with beading and gilded triangles (*54, 81*). The bowl of the ladle had been detached from its handle and driven on to the base-ring of the great silver dish, where it was stuck fast, by the weight that fell on the dish when the burial chamber collapsed. The driving-in of its rim under pressure from the base-rim of the Anastasius dish can be clearly seen (*54*). Inside the smaller silver dish were a number of small globular vessels with silver-gilt rims decorated with animal ornament (*48*). The cups are made from burr wood, that is, bulbous growths on a tree, in this case walnut (*57–59*). Below the smaller silver dish were the remains of a 'leather bag'. Other objects beneath the great dish were the remains of several pairs of leather shoes, an ivory gaming piece, three bone combs (inside the fluted bowl), a small cup apparently of horn and two more hanging-bowls with decorated escutcheons, smaller than the one previously mentioned, but both of great interest (*55, 56*). Lying in folds at the bottom of this deposit was a mass of rusted iron mail, the remains of a mail coat. Radiography of the rusted mass shows that the rows of rings were alternately riveted and welded. In the riveted rows the ends of each ring were hammered into a spatulate shape, made to overlap, and fastened with a minute copper rivet. As the folds had rusted into a solid lump it is not possible to reconstruct the shape or size of the original garment or to say, for example, whether it had sleeves. No buckles or other metal fittings that might possibly have been associated with a coat of mail were revealed in the radiographic survey.

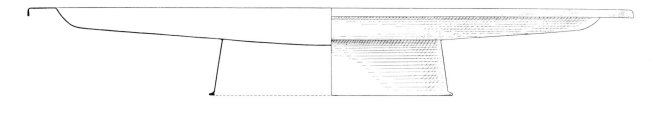

46 *Sectional drawing of the Anastasius dish. (Scale, approximately 1/4)*

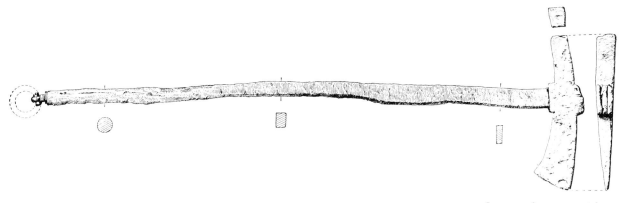

47 *Iron axe-hammer, with iron handle ending in two rings. From beneath the Anastasius dish. (Scale, 1/7)*

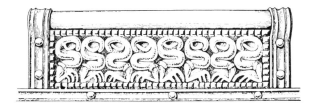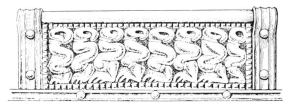

48 *Panels of animal ornament from the rims of two of the burr-wood cups. (Scale, 3/2)*

The whole of this complex of finds under the Anastasius dish was found to have been placed on a 'round wooden platter or tray'. The comparatively good preservation of the perishables in it was no doubt due to its having been compressed by the weight of the collapsed mound between the great dish and this 'tray', and also physically sheltered by the great dish from the disintegrating effects of drainage.

49–51 *The Anastasius dish, and control stamps of two types from beneath the base. (Scales, dish slightly under 1/5; the stamps enlarged)*

52 *Remains of bronze cauldrons, iron-bound wooden bucket, iron chain work and great silver dish as uncovered in the ground. The silver bowl with classical head (53) can be seen projecting from under the great silver dish.*

53 *Fluted silver bowl with classical head in the tondo, and the handles detached. (Scale, about 1/3) See also 82 for detail.*

Opposite, top:
54 (a) *Silver cup*; (b)
bowl from handled silver ladle.
(Scale, 1/1)
Opposite, bottom:
55, 56 *Details from the*
second and third hanging
bowls. **55,** *from the base of*
bowl no. 2 (Scale 4/5); **56,**
escutcheon and ring from bowl
no. 3 (Scale, 2/1)

Top to bottom:
57–59 *Small cup made from*
burr-wood, with fluted silver-
gilt rim, and similar rims with
animal ornament or flutes
from other burr-wood cups.
(Scales, 1/1)

Pottery Bottle

To south of the great dish complex was a small wheel-turned pottery bottle of buff ware (60). Its only decorative feature is a light groove running three times round the body. The use of the wheel suggests that it was an import into East Anglia.

60 *Pottery bottle. (Scale, about actual size)*

Iron Lamp

Farther to the east was a rusted iron object which suggested a hemispherical cup on a stem with three legs. It appeared to be partitioned internally, and was thought by the excavators to be probably a lamp, like that found in a Saxon barrow at Broomfield, Essex,[30] now in the British Museum, but in this case with divisions for several wicks. The internal partitions, however, were only rust-formations that had developed in radial cracks in the contained matter. This was a hard cake of whitish substance which has been identified as bees' wax, a fact which substantiates identification as a lamp. The lamp, its features elucidated as far as possible through mechanical cleaning, is illustrated together with its close parallel from the Broomfield barrow (61).

61 *Iron tripod lamp from the Sutton Hoo ship-burial* (left) *with a cake of beeswax* (centre) *found inside the bowl; with* (right) *the iron tripod lamp from the barrow at Broomfield, Essex, for comparison. (Scale, slightly under 1/3)*

OBJECTS DEPOSITED ACROSS
THE EAST END OF THE BURIAL CHAMBER

Bronze Cauldrons and Iron Chain-work Complex (52)

Ranged against the east wall of the chamber were (from north to south): the very fragmentary remains of a large iron-bound wooden tub, or bucket, 64 in. (160 cm) in circumference (64), reconstructed, on a fibre-glass shape replacing the wood, by Mr Nigel Williams, formerly one of the Department's Conservation Officers, and of a large bronze cauldron; a mass of badly rusted iron, which disintegrated during war-time storage, consisting of an elaboration of massive rings, chains and bars, a gear for suspending the cauldron; a lesser bronze cauldron and a third smaller example, both the latter smashed and corroded beyond restoration. The design of the chain-work has been recovered in full as a result of much very skilful work by two of the Museum staff, Mrs Valerie Fenwick, who worked out the design, and Mr P. G. T. Shorer, who reassembled and built up the hundreds of disintegrated fragments to which the iron had been reduced during war-time evacuation (62, 63). With the cauldron suspended, the whole was about 12 ft 6 in. (about 3.75 m) in length, and of an unparalleled elaboration. Similar but smaller and less complex or ornate suspension chains occur in a number of Romano-British finds,[30] and iron suspension-gear, much less ambitious, but showing similarities, also occurs in Swedish boat-graves and in Viking contexts.[31] A modern reconstruction (63), based on drawings worked out in the British Museum, was executed by the Sussex blacksmiths, Messrs Landon of Crowborough.

OTHER FEATURES OF THE BURIAL DEPOSIT

Grave goods lying outside the main formation

Well to the south of the keel-line, and nearly half-way along the burial-chamber from the west wall, where the remains of a third iron-bound wooden bucket (7). North of this were three iron ferrules, belonging to the angons whose heads were thrust through one of the handles of the bronze Coptic bowl at the west end of the chamber. Some 18 in. (46 cm) to the south of the sword-hilt a rather shapeless length of heavily rusted iron represented the blade of a large hunting spear.[32] Radiography reveals no decorative features.

Evidence for the Construction of the Burial Chamber

The remains of boards found overlying the burial deposit were recovered in the 1939 excavations. These boards ran in two directions.

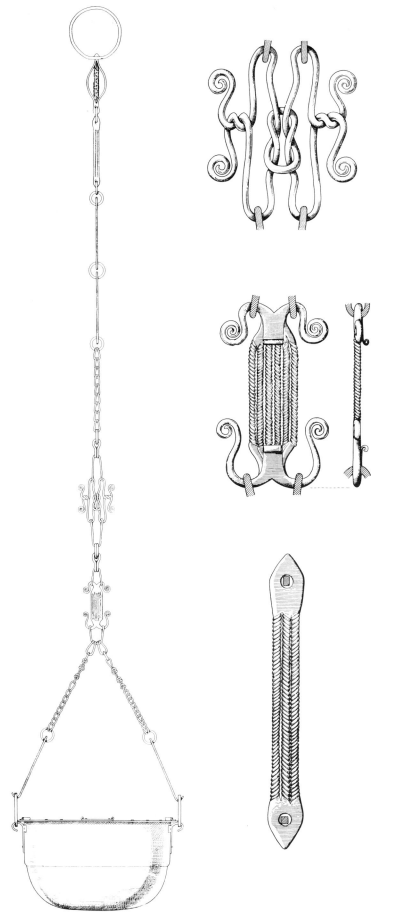

62 *The elaborate wrought-iron suspension-gear associated with the largest bronze cauldron seen overall and in three details of the elements. From the east end of the burial chamber. Drawings based on the reconstruction of the chainwork by Mrs Valerie Fenwick. (Scales, overall 1/16; details 1/4)*

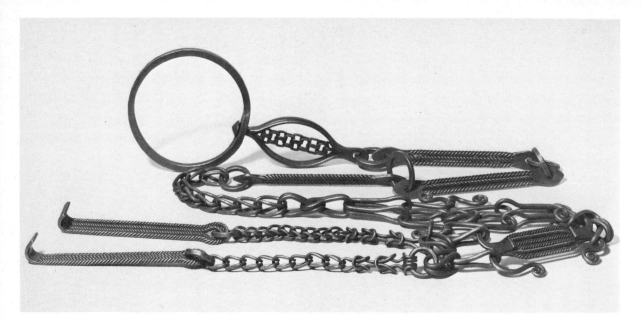

63 *Elaborate wrought-iron suspension-gear associated with the largest cauldron. Replica made by F. Landon Crowborough, Sussex.*

64 *Reconstruction of the iron-bound wooden tub. (Scale, 1/5)*

They were probably from the roof of the collapsed chamber, and suggested that it was constructed of a double thickness of wood, with the two layers laid at right angles to each other. A system of iron cleats was also found in 1939, running in roughly parallel lines along either side of the chamber. These cleats or fitments occurred only within the area of the burial chamber and may have been connected with its construction. They must originally have been set in straight alignments, the disarrangement shown in the plan being due to the distortion and collapse of the chamber. The cleats did not, however, extend to the ends of the chamber and might possibly be connected with the building of a platform or table within the burial-chamber, on which the grave goods along the keel-line may have been laid out. They might also have been connected with a construction for carrying a mast.

The Body

Careful scrutiny by the experienced excavators revealed no trace or sign of human remains, either cremated or inhumed, in the body space (see p. 23). The absence there of intimately personal objects, such as the dead man's finger-ring or pendant, and of pins, tags, buckles, or gold thread, that might have survived from shoes and clothing, or a shroud; and the lack of convincing arrangement of sword, jewellery, and other normally worn objects with relation to a body in any posture, could also be considered as indicating that no body had ever been laid in the grave. The grave had not been disturbed so that the body could not have been removed later, as was the case with the Gokstad, Oseberg and Ladby ship-burials. But the absence of personalia may not be decisive and it is quite possible, in appropriate conditions, for acid sand, such as this was (pH 4.5), to eliminate all traces of a body, even the teeth. Because of this possibility, a series of intricate chemical tests has been carried out on the grave goods and other remains from the burial chamber, and to this evidence obtained in re-excavation of the burial-chamber in 1965–67 can be added. The results suggest that there may well have been a body after all along the keel-line between the drinking-horn complex and the sceptre, flanked by the sword and helmet. Certainly there was a major phosphate source near the sword. At the same time, the original presence of cremated bone, in some quantity, on or above the Anastasius dish, has also been demonstrated.[33] It is impossible to say whether this calcined bone source, of which only casts and chemical indications have survived, was animal (possibly remains of a funeral feast or of sacrificed animals) or human. No fragments of burnt-up grave goods, such as are normally found with bone remains gathered up from the funeral pyre, were found here on the Anastasius dish. Equally, it cannot be shown whether the high phosphate source in the sword region was human or animal, though it must have had a skeletal origin. The issues are complicated, but it seems highly unlikely that the chemical traces on the silver dish which can, it seems, only have been derived from cremated or charred bone, represent a human burial in the ship.[34] The grave may have been an orthodox burial, and the bones on the dish remains of a funeral feast or of barbecued viands (to account for the presence of carbon traces). The significance of these possibilities is discussed in Chapter VII.

In a re-excavation of the burial-chamber by the writer in 1967 considerable fragments of a creamy-white phosphatic material were recovered from the area between the positions of the shield and helmet. Two minute splinters of ivory were also found in the area. These phosphatic remains are probably due to a set of draughtsmen. Fragments of gaming-pieces of ivory, found in 1939, came from this area of the burial-deposit.[35] If this identification is accepted, it would be likely that the burial-deposit had included a set, which would quite probably have amounted to thirty or forty pieces. It seems, however, that the distribution of the (scattered) ivory gaming pieces was such that they alone cannot account for the heavy phosphatic impregnation of the sword. Some other major source must have existed here, and this may have been a human body.

It should be noted that, although there was plenty of unused space in the burial chamber to either side of the keel-line, no remains were found of sacrificed animals, such as horses and dogs, as were regularly deposited in contemporary Swedish ship-burials and cremations. Nor were remains found of sacrificed slaves or other persons, in addition to sacrificed animals, as are sometimes found in graves of the Viking Age.[36]

CHAPTER III

The excavation of the ship and a reconstruction of the burial

The frontispiece gives a view of the excavated ship, with the burial deposit removed, looking towards the stern. As has already been said (p. 19) the fore-part of the ship, from the bows (*69*) to the burial chamber, had been exposed by Mr Basil Brown before Mr Phillips took charge. The fact that it was possible to obtain such complete pictorial records and impressions of the ship and to recover its general features in full (see Chapter IV, *70*) was due to the flair and caution with which Mr Brown, to whom great credit is due, carried out this earlier part of the operation, as well as to very judicious subsequent excavation.

The section (*65*) shows the ship in its approximate relation to its mound and to ground level. It also shows the position and conjectural form of the burial chamber and shows that the ship fitted very closely into its trench. In *66* the ship is shown in plan in relation to its mound but not to the trench in which it was buried, although the limits of this were approximately fixed. The mound was circular and when re-excavated in 1968–69 by Mr Paul Ashbee, FSA, was found to have measured originally 106 ft from NE to SW and 96 ft from NW to SE, as compared with surveyed dimensions of 100 ft by 110 ft for mound 2 (*2*). Mound 1, if of less diameter, may have been somewhat higher than Mound 2. It was certainly considered in 1938 to be the largest of the group. The appearance of extra height may, however, have been enhanced by the lowering of the surrounding surfaces, deturfed for the mound-building, a procedure apparently not followed in building Mound 2. The new section (*65*) gives a maximum height above the pre-barrow ground surface of 9 ft (approx. 2.75 m).

A Reconstruction of the Burial

To play its part in the burial, the ship, nearly 90 ft long and 14 ft in the beam (about 27 m long and 4.25 m wide) was hauled overland more

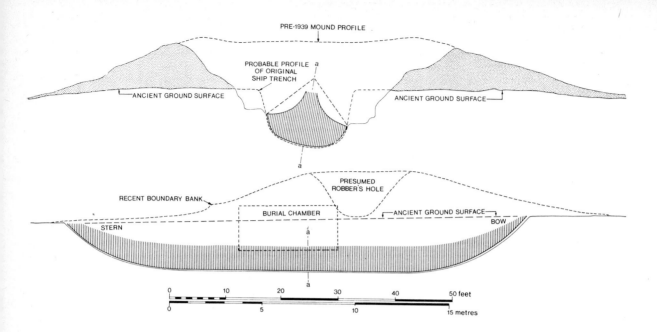

PRE-1939 MOUND PROFILE

PROBABLE PROFILE
OF ORIGINAL
SHIP TRENCH

ANCIENT GROUND SURFACE

ANCIENT GROUND SURFACE

PRESUMED
ROBBER'S HOLE

RECENT BOUNDARY BANK

BURIAL CHAMBER

ANCIENT GROUND SURFACE

STERN

BOW

0   10   20   30   40   50 feet

0   5   10   15 metres

65   *Two sections through the ship-barrow, based on fresh excavation of the mound in 1967–69.*

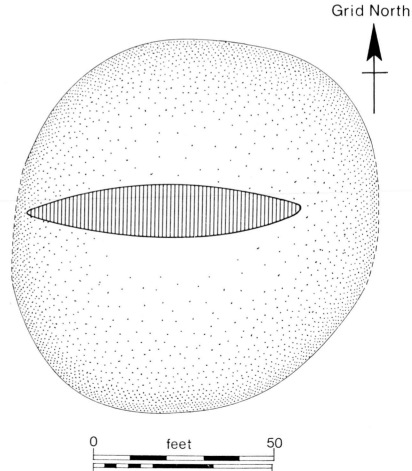

Grid North

66   *Diagram showing the Sutton Hoo ship in relation to the mound, based on fresh survey and excavation by Paul Ashbee, FSA, in 1967–69.*

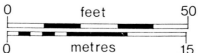

0   feet   50

0   metres   15

than a third of a mile from the estuary, and a hundred feet up on the edge of the escarpment, bow foremost. Here a trench was dug to receive it. The ship was pushed forward on rollers until it rested immediately over the trench. It was lifted by pulling on ropes passed under its keel and over bollards ranged along either side. The rollers were then withdrawn and the ship lowered slowly and evenly into its grave. A strongly constructed wooden cabin, with end-walls and high-pitched gabled roof, its eaves running over the tops of the gunwales, was erected amidships. The burial deposit was laid out in it and strewn with bracken. This practice has also been observed in Viking-ship burials in Norway. The sand that had been excavated to make the trench for the boat was then filled back into the space between the edges of the trench and the sides of the ship, and into the boat itself, so that the ship's timbers were imprisoned in solid sand. Finally the ground was levelled off and a mound, made from material from the surrounding heath, was built up over the ship.[37] Elaborate rituals no doubt accompanied these operations, but what they were we can only infer from early literary accounts of similar burials. There was no clear archaeological evidence on this point,[38] and nothing relevant emerged when the portions of the mound that remained intact after the 1939 excavation to the north and south of the ship-trench were excavated in 1968 and 1969.

The foregoing reconstruction of the funeral operations is based on observations made by Mr Phillips in the course of the excavations. The close fit of the ship in its burial-trench, referred to above, and the fact that the trench was closed at either end (i.e. there was no sloping ramp leading to it) was thought to imply a controlled lowering of the ship into its grave.

Visitors to the Museum may be surprised to see that no ship, nor any portion of one, is on exhibition. All that remained in the burial-mound, however, when opened by the excavators, were the iron rivets that once held the ship's timbers together, each rivet still in position, and a ship-shaped system of stains in the sand where the timbers had been. By carefully removing sand from the inside until they reached and exposed the roves and stained layer, however, the excavators were able to recover the exact shape of the ship and to take its lines, except at the stem and stern, fully and accurately.

In the frontispiece the roves (small diamond-shaped plates on which the rivet-ends were clenched) can be seen in long alignments, and the vertical spikes that fastened the thole-bases to the gunwale strake (71) can be seen at intervals down either side of the ship. The excavators found the sand wet and firm, and it was because the ship's timbers were held fast in well-packed sand that the nails and bolts, outside the burial-chamber area at any rate, remained exactly in position, when the timbers disintegrated.

The Burial Chamber

The length of the burial chamber was given by thin lines of stain crossing the ship at either end of the burial deposit. They marked the position of the wooden end-walls and were $17\frac{1}{2}$ ft (6.75 m) apart. Similarly, the fact that there was originally a gabled wooden roof over the burial deposit was indicated to the excavators by thin sloping lines of discoloration in the sand, well above the deposit. These sloping lines also gave the approximate original angle of pitch of the roof. The fact that the bottom edges of this roof rested over the gunwales was indicated by the sectional drawings made of these appearances at the time.

An earlier attempt to rob the grave

A treasure-hunter's hole was dug into the top of the mound (65). Fortunately the centre of the mound, due to the digging away of its western end, which evidently occurred before the attempt, was no longer directly above the burial deposit. This, and the difficulty of digging a deep hole in loose sand, made the attempt a failure. The treasure-hunters seem to have had a meal in the bottom of their hole, where animal bones and the remains of a fire were found, with a piece of tigerware jug, which dated this episode to the later sixteenth or beginning of the seventeenth century.

Opposite:
67 *Excavators at work in the ship in 1967.*

CHAPTER IV

The ship

The Sutton Hoo ship (frontispiece and *70*) was a great open rowing boat, some 80 ft long as traced in the ground. Its original overall length may be estimated at 89 ft (27 m) as compared with the approximate 79, 69

68   The Sutton Hoo ship under sail, a reconstruction by Harold Åkerlund, drawn by H. Schösler-Pedersen (by permission of Harold Åkerlund and Erlanders Boktrykeri Aktiebolag, Göteborg, and the editor of Søens Verden)

and 68 ft (24, 21 and 20.7 m) of the Gokstad, Oseberg and Ladby Viking ships respectively. It is the longest vessel yet found from the migration period or the later Viking age. Its greatest beam was 14 ft (4.25 m) and its depth amidships 4 ft 6 in. (1.37 m). The prow rose to a height of at least 12½ ft (3.8 m) above the level of the keel-plank amidships. It drew 2 ft (0.6 m) of water when light. It was clinker-built, with nine strakes a side, apparently without permanent decking. The hull was stiffened with twenty-six ribs which were attached to the skin of the ship by wooden pegs and, at gunwale level, by a heavy iron bolt. The boat was driven by forty oarsmen.[39] No indication was found of a mast or other provision for sailing, but it is thought that a vessel of such breadth and strength might well have employed sail with following winds, in spite of the absence, as it seems, of any proper keel. A reconstruction by the Swedish ship expert Harald Åkerlund of the Sutton Hoo ship as it would appear under sail is shown in *68*. The ship was of some age when buried, since the hull showed considerable traces of repair. It had not been stove in or deliberately damaged by the funeral party.

A suggested reconstruction of the gunwale and upper strakes (*71*), shows them from the inside between ribs 19 and 20 port. This drawing is based on a photograph taken by the Science Museum in 1939.

The ship was steered over the stern by a large steering-oar, or side rudder, as in the case of the Nydam and Gokstad ships, and as seen

69 *View of the bow of the ship. Its projection above the old ground surface, subsequently covered up by barrow-material, may be seen.*

in carved representations on standing stones of the era, from the Baltic island of Gotland and elsewhere. The rib-formation hereabouts had been strengthened to take extra strain on the starboard side. The steersman probably stood on a small platform at this point, and controlled the steering oar by means of an athwartship tiller stepped in its upper end. There was a similar arrangement for steering the well-known Nydam ship (about AD 400) found in Schleswig in 1863 in a peat bog

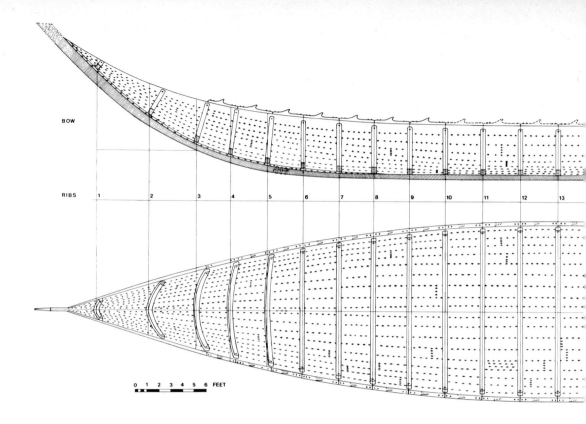

BOW

RIBS   1   2   3   4   5   6   7   8   9   10   11   12   13

0 1 2 3 4 5 6 FEET

70 *Archaeological reconstruction of the ship.*

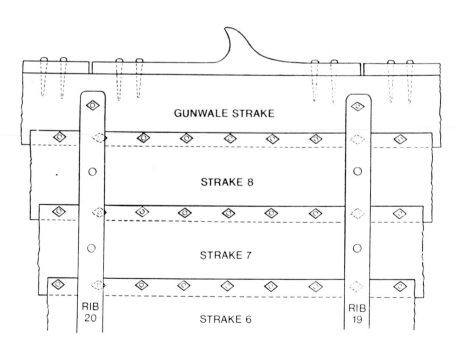

GUNWALE STRAKE

STRAKE 8

STRAKE 7

RIB 20   STRAKE 6   RIB 19

71 *Reconstruction of the gunwale and upper strakes of the Sutton Hoo ship between ribs 19 and 20 port, seen from the inside. (Based on a photograph taken by the Science Museum in 1939.)*

0   1   2   3 feet

0   1 metre

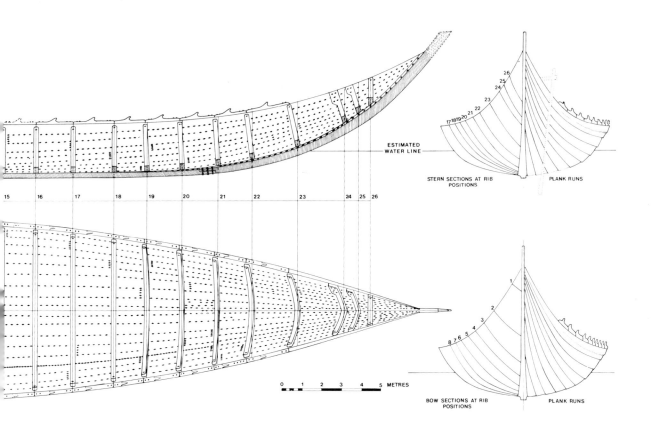

ESTIMATED
WATER LINE

STERN SECTIONS AT RIB
POSITIONS

PLANK RUNS

BOW SECTIONS AT RIB
POSITIONS

PLANK RUNS

0 1 2 3 4 5 METRES

with timbers preserved. The Nydam ship is now exhibited in the Nydam
and Thorsberg Hall in the Schleswig-Holsteinisches Landesmuseum
für Vor- und Frühgeschichte, in Schloss Gottorp, Schleswig.

A technical advance in the Sutton Hoo ship as compared with the
Nydam ship is that the strakes are each made up of several lengths of
timber riveted together at overlapping joints, or scarfs. This shows an
increased confidence in technique, for the Nydam builders had used,
in a primitive manner, continuous pieces of wood, up to 73 ft (22 m)
long (the maximum length of the hull), so that the whole of the hull
of their vessel, excluding the internal framework, consisted of only
seventeen pieces of wood. In the Sutton Hoo ship, as in the Nydam
ship, however, strakes are still relatively broad and few. In the later Viking ships (which were often ocean-going vessels propelled by sails as
well as oars) strakes are narrower and almost twice as numerous. The
Gokstad ship has sixteen strakes a side. An element of refinement of
the construction of the Sutton Hoo ship is that the strakes in this large
vessel were only one inch thick. This is indicated by the length of the
plank joint pins where the ends of abutting lengths of strake were scarfed
and overlapped. The standard rivets which fastened overlapping strakes
show a distance of approximately two inches between the domed head

and the rove, thus accommodating the overlap that occurs of two one-inch planks.

Up to the present, only three boats of the pagan Saxon period, if we leave aside the small portions of boats found by Mr Charles Green at Caister-on-Sea (1) in use as lids over burials or to cradle the bodies, have been identified in England. All come from this small corner of the Suffolk coast. They are the two, already discussed, from Sutton Hoo, and a third from Snape, on the River Alde, ten miles to the north (1). The remains of this last ship, some 50 ft (15.25 m) in length, were found in 1862.[40] Of these three vessels, the Sutton Hoo ship is much the largest and most impressive. It was longer than the Nydam ship, longer than the longest of the Viking ships yet found, and much larger than the boats, built for lakes and inland waterways, excavated at the Swedish sites at Vendel and Valsgärde, north of Stockholm. It comes to us from a period of our history, the pagan phase of the Anglo-Saxons, whose archaeological remains, it has been said, comprise nothing 'larger than a bucket or longer than a sword'.[41] This picture is modified by recent discoveries, in post-hole plans of timber halls and other buildings, and by the burial mounds themselves. But the Sutton Hoo ship nevertheless ranks as among the most important monuments of our sixth and seventh century pagan ancestors that have yet come down to us. Since it is relatively closely dated (around 600 AD) and since careful excavation has recovered most of its detail, it is also a highly important document in the history of shipping and ship-construction.

It is sad that, as is almost invariably the case with buried ships, the upper parts or terminations of the stem and stern posts did not survive, even as soil-impressions, or vestigially. Some clue to the nature of such stem and stern posts in a royal vessel at this early date would have been very welcome and might have given us valuable information about the standards then prevailing in the largely lost but important art of wood carving. Two ships' figure heads recently assigned to this period or earlier by Carbon 14 dating give some idea of what might have been expected.[42]

CHAPTER V

The nature of the burial and parallels to it

The objects found in the Sutton Hoo ship are the remains of a funeral deposit. They are useful things intended for the convenience of the dead person in a life beyond the grave, where, in the pagan view, the individual's needs would be much the same as in this life. He would need money, his weapons and armour, his utensils, his personal symbols and ornaments.[43] The 'grave goods' were also intended to signalize his status in his society. He would travel on the journey to the next world in his ship and as a king. Deposition of grave goods in accordance with such ideas was the universal practice of the pagan Germans, as of their prehistoric predecessors, as the innumerable barrows of our landscape bear witness. The possibility that a body may not have been buried with the grave goods may only mean that the body, for some reason, could not be buried, and does not make it any the less a funeral deposit. The unsurpassed richness of the grave goods, and other factors, such as the objects, like the iron stand and ceremonial stone, interpreted as symbols of office, leave no doubt that the burial is that of a royal person. The fact that the barrow is one of a group of fifteen or more strongly suggests that this royal person was buried among his ancestors in a family burial-ground.

A pagan royal burial-ground, if the Sutton Hoo grave field proves to be such, would be without parallel in early Germanic archaeology outside Scandinavia. Contemporary parallels, however, both for the family cemetery and for the practice of ship-burial at a lower social level, are to be found at the two Swedish sites already mentioned, Vendel and Valsgärde, on the River Fyris in the Uppland province, a short distance to the north of Uppsala, which in turn lies to the north of Stockholm. Here the series of successive burials seems to begin at about the time of the Sutton Hoo interment, or, since the early dating of the Sutton Hoo grave is now established, perhaps a little later.

Ship-burial is described in a famous passage, describing the funeral of the Danish King Scyld, in the earliest European epic poem outside the classical tongues, the Anglo-Saxon *Beowulf*. It is generally held that *Beowulf* was written down in England, around the year AD 700 or somewhat later, that is, seventy or more years after the burial of the Sutton Hoo ship; but the poem describes events of an earlier period. The passage, in a new translation by Mr Kevin Crossley-Holland, is as follows:[44]

> Then Scyld departed at the destined hour,
> that powerful man sought the Lord's protection.
> His own close companions carried him
> down to the sea, as he, Lord of the Danes,
> had asked while he could still speak.
> That well-loved man had ruled his land for many years.
> There in the harbour stood the ring-prowed ship,
> the prince's vessel, shrouded in ice and eager to sail;
> and then they laid their dear lord,
> the giver of rings, deep within the ship
> by the mast in majesty; many treasures
> and adornments from far and wide were gathered there.
> I have never heard of a ship equipped
> more handsomely with weapons and war-gear,
> swords and corslets; on his breast
> lay countless treasures that were to travel far
> with him into the waves' domain.
> They gave him great ornaments, gifts
> no less magnificent than those men had given him
> long before, when they sent him alone,
> child as he was, across the stretch of the seas.[45]
> Then high above his head they placed
> a golden banner and let the waves bear him,
> bequeathed him to the sea; their hearts were grieving,
> their minds mourning. Mighty men
> beneath the heavens, rulers in the hall,
> cannot say who received that cargo.

Another passage describes the funeral of Beowulf himself. This was not a ship-burial, but the passage tells us how the great were buried, how mounds were built over the remains, and what sort of funeral rites accompanied the interment. The most relevant lines are as follows:

> Then, on the headland, the Geats prepared a mighty pyre
> for Beowulf, hung round with helmets and shields
> and shining mail, in accordance with his wishes;
> and then the mourning warriors laid
> their dear lord, the famous prince, upon it.
> And there, on Whaleness, the heroes kindled
> the most mighty of pyres; the dark wood-smoke
> soared over the fire, the roaring flames
> mingled with weeping—the winds' tumult subsided—
> until the body became ash, consumed even
> to its core ...

Then the Geats built a barrow on the headland—
it was high and broad, visible from far
to all seafarers; in ten days they built the beacon
for that courageous man; and they constructed
as noble an enclosure as wise men
could devise, to enshrine the ashes.
They buried rings and brooches in the barrow,
all those adornments that brave men
had brought out from the hoard after Beowulf died.
They bequeathed the gleaming gold, treasure of men,
to the earth, and there it was before.
Then twelve brave warriors, sons of heroes,
rode round the barrow, sorrowing;
they mourned their king, chanted
an elegy, spoke about that great man:
They exalted his heroic life, lauded
his daring deeds.
Thus the Geats, his hearth-companions,
grieved over the death of their lord;
they said that of all kings on earth
he was the kindest, the most gentle,
the most just to his people, the most eager for fame.[46]

These passages make the significance of the Sutton Hoo burial clear. True, in the first, the funeral ship was not buried, but set out to sea, and in the second, the body, and armour and weapons with it, were cremated, and precious things are then said to have been added to the ashes of the pyre after the burning, and before the tumulus was raised, a practice unknown to archaeology and appearing in the poem perhaps as the result of some confusion of tradition. But allowing for these differences, we may assume that similar ceremonies took place in the earlier part of the seventh century, by the waters of the Suffolk Deben.

These literary accounts make it plain that the Sutton Hoo treasures were not buried in secret. They also make it plain that those who buried the treasures did not intend to recover them later. It was these two considerations which led the Suffolk jurors, in accordance with English law, to find that the gold and silver in the ship were not Treasure Trove.[47] However, apart from these passages, it is clear that the burial must have been public knowledge. A considerable labour force must have been employed to drag the ship half a mile from the river, to lower it into its trench, and to erect the tumulus.

CHAPTER VI

The coins and the date of the burial

In the purse there were found thirty-seven small gold coins, three unstruck circular blanks, and two small ingots, all of gold (*75*). The coins are all of Continental origin, and all struck at mints located in the lands occupied or controlled at that time by the Merovingian Franks; that is, generally speaking, within the area comprised by modern France, Belgium, the Rhineland and Switzerland (*74*). They vary in weight between extremes of 1.059 and 1.389 gm, in diameter between 10 and 15 mm. The obverses of all but two of them (nos. 34 and 36; *75*) carry heads, stylized or degenerate in various degrees. The reverses in all but three cases (nos. 35 and 36, a chalice, and 37, a monogram) carry variants of the theme of a cross on a globe or on steps, or an equal-armed cross. Only one coin, no. 2, a coin struck at Clermont-Ferrand, can be identified with a king, the Frankish king Theodebert II (AD 595–612).

Knowledge of Merovingian coinage has only very recently in respect of dating reached a stage of some precision. This coinage presents difficulties, both in identifying and localizing the mints and in dating. The flans, or blank metal discs which when struck become coins, were often too small for the die, so that only the bottoms of the letters of the legends register. Sometimes dies continue in use after wear or damage. Legends are sometimes retrograde, that is, the die was incorrectly cut (not reversed) so that the letters on the coin have to be read backwards. Sometimes these partial and often largely erased letters have to be read backwards and upside down as well. In consequence, legends on thirty per cent of Merovingian coins are illegible, or only legible with great difficulty or uncertainty. Those which can be read generally carry the name of the town of issue or the mint on one face, and that of the moneyer or mint-master on the other.

Almost every sizeable town or large village, some churches, and various royal establishments, had their own mints. Over 2000 of these are known, and even when the place-name on the coin can be read, it is sometimes impossible, or difficult with assurance, to identify it with a modern place, and so locate the mint. A great deal of work has been

Opposite: *72* *Replica of a maplewood bottle with silver and gold rim-mounts, one of a set of six. (Scale, approximately 5/4)*

73 *One of the pair
of golden shoulder clasps
decorated with cloisonné
garnets and* millefiore *glass,
with the fastening pin
withdrawn (Scale, 5/4)*

done on mint and moneyer identifications, chiefly in two great comprehensive catalogues published in 1892–95;[48] these studies are both 70 years old and there is much revision to be done. This is now being accomplished by M. Jean Lafaurie, at the Cabinet des Médailles in the Bibliothèque Nationale in Paris, where the bulk of surviving Merovingian gold coins is to be found. Relatively little attention has, however, been paid, until recently, to the chronology of the series. Some coins like no. 2 in the Sutton Hoo hoard bear the names of identifiable kings, and these and certain others, like those with the name of the moneyer Eligius who became Bishop of Noyon (probably St Eloi, the patron saint of goldsmiths), whose name appears on the issues of three kings, Clothair II (613–29), Dagobert I (622–38) and Clovis II (639–57), offer a few fixed points in dating. But with so many mints striking simultaneously, and so many designs being perpetually copied and re-copied, or revised, with varying degrees of skill or comprehension, the dating of Merovingian coins has been a matter of great uncertainty. Style as a criterion of date can only be used with the greatest circumspection.

Until 1960, a firm consensus of opinion had grown up among the few numismatists specializing in this field, including M. Lafaurie, that the thirty-seven gold coins in the Sutton Hoo purse must have come together sometime in the decade AD 650–60.[49] In 1960, however, M. Lafaurie, in the course of a general revision of the accepted chronological framework of Merovingian gold coins,[50] put the assembly of the Sutton Hoo hoard much earlier, about AD 625. His work has been subjected to some detailed criticism, but his general position is now supported, on other grounds, by Dr J. P. C. Kent, of the Department of Coins and Medals, British Museum, who has recently completed the definitive study of the Sutton Hoo coins, with the special assignment of establishing the date of the hoard. Dr Kent's verdict of 'not later than 630 for any coin; and 625 as the likely date for the assembly'[51] agrees generally with that of M. Lafaurie, and his work establishes the new early trend in the dating of the Merovingian series. The basis of Dr Kent's new chronology of the Merovingian gold coinage is metallurgical analysis of over eight hundred examples, including almost all coins bearing kings' names and so datable within the regnal limits. This has enabled a precise chronological framework to be applied to the process of debasement known to have characterised this currency increasingly in the course of the seventh century.

With a find so significant as the Sutton Hoo burial, a variation of thirty or forty years in the date of deposition makes a great difference. With such a margin of error it becomes impossible to draw the firm conclusions that might otherwise be drawn on many crucial issues of the century. At a period when so very little of our cultural inheritance can be precisely dated, great importance attaches to the few landmarks that

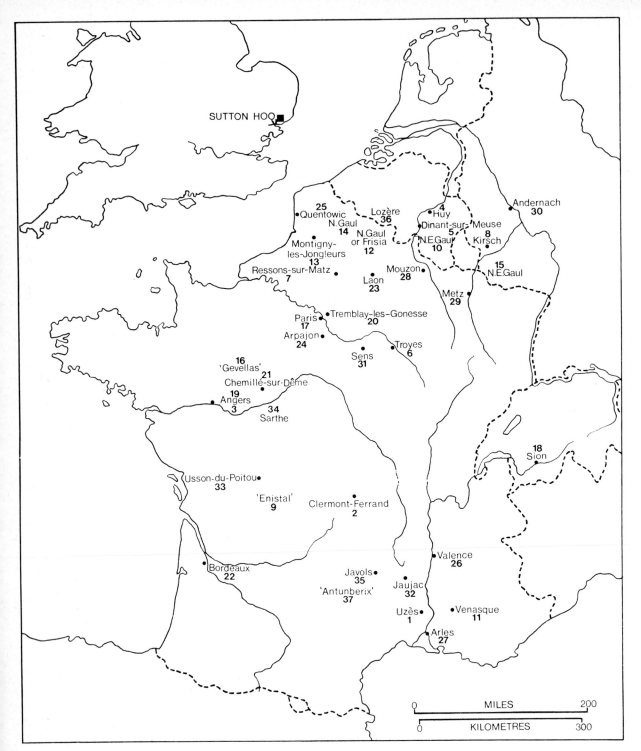

SUTTON HOO

25
Quentowic
N.Gaul

Lozère
36

4
Huy
Dinant-sur-Meuse
5
N.E.Gaul
10

Andernach
30

8
Kirsch

14
N.Gaul
or Frisia
12

Montigny-
les-Jongleurs
13

Ressons-sur-Matz
7

Mouzon
28

15
N.E.Gaul

Laon
23

Metz
29

Paris
17

Tremblay-les-Gonesse
20

Arpajon
24

Troyes
6

Sens
31

16
'Gevellas'

21
Chemillé-sur-Dême

19
Angers
3

34
Sarthe

18
Sion

Usson-du-Poitou
33

'Enistal'
9

Clermont-Ferrand
2

Valence
26

Bordeaux
22

Javols
35

Jaujac
32

'Antunberix'
37

Uzès
1

Venasque
11

Arles
27

MILES
0   200

KILOMETRES
0   300

74 *Map showing the locations of mints at*
which coins found in the purse in the Sutton
Hoo ship-burial were struck. (Based on mint-
identifications by Allen, Grierson and
Lafaurie.) See also 75.

can. The richer and the more significant these are, the greater the historical value of being able to date them.

A further point has to be borne in mind. The date at which the coins were brought together to form the assemblage found in the purse is one thing. The date when it was buried may be another. Hoards normally are hidden by their possessors, usually merchants, in the face of sudden danger. Such hoards, in their place of burial and their contents, reflect the state of the merchant's trade, or at least betray something of its nature, at the actual moment of burial. Such hoards invariably contain concentrations of coins struck at the same mint. Thus the Escharen hoard, an analysis of which is the basis of M. Lafaurie's new chronology, included out of sixty coins, apart from isolated outliers from widely scattered mints, seventeen from one unknown mint on the lower Rhine, all struck from the same dies; six from Bonn; six from Cologne, and seven from another mint on the Rhine, near Nijmegen. The hoard itself was buried at Escharen, close to the river, and not far from Nijmegen. The picture it presents is a clear one of trade primarily with the Rhineland and Frisia. In all such cases (i.e. of merchants' hoards) it is safe to infer that the burial of the coins took place very soon indeed after their coming together.

The Sutton Hoo hoard, exceptionally, is not a merchant's hoard. Of seventeen hoards of Merovingian coins at present known it is the only large assembly to have been found in a grave, and the grave is a king's grave, containing gifts and heirlooms. It is likely that East Anglia, especially at the early period now assigned by Kent and Lafaurie to the coins, lay outside the limited area of southern England where coins were minted, or circulated as currency. The hoard may have had the nature of a treasure, rather than representing coin in circulation or trade at the time of the burial.

It is an odd fact also that no two of the thirty-seven coins in this king's grave come from the same mint. The hoard contains no concentrations, however small. It is almost as though the coins had been hand-picked somewhere, at some stage (not necessarily at the time of the funeral) to represent as many different types and mints as possible. No doubt the latest available when the selection was made would be included. If, however, the hoard had been at some time brought or sent over from the Continent as a gift or part of a diplomatic payment, the absence from it of later types circulating on the Continent cannot be used with assurance as grounds for depressing the date of its burial in Suffolk. The hoard might, as a gift, have been kept intact for some years, or have been extracted from a larger group of coins that had been kept unreplenished for some years, before it came to be relinquished to the soil at a king's death. So there are considerations which made it necessary in the Sutton Hoo instance to bear in mind the distinction between the

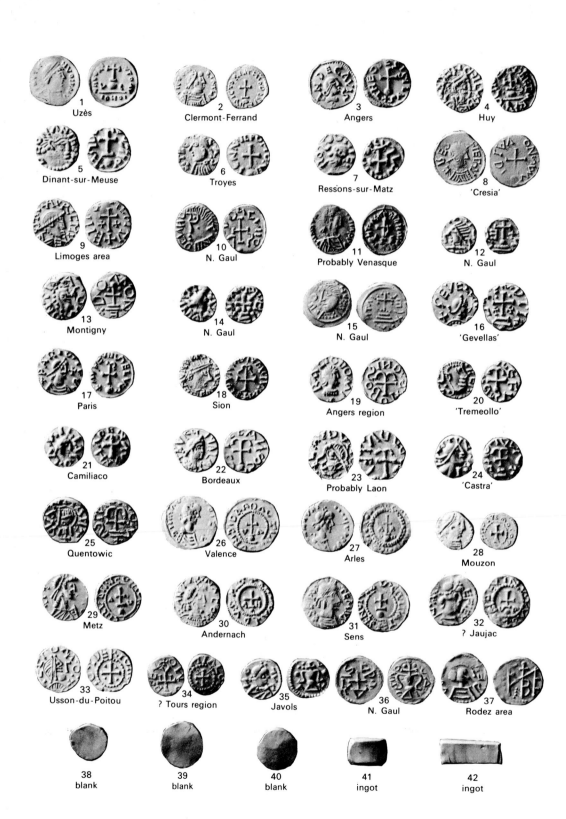

1
Uzès

2
Clermont-Ferrand

3
Angers

4
Huy

5
Dinant-sur-Meuse

6
Troyes

7
Ressons-sur-Matz

8
'Cresia'

9
Limoges area

10
N. Gaul

11
Probably Venasque

12
N. Gaul

13
Montigny

14
N. Gaul

15
N. Gaul

16
'Gevellas'

17
Paris

18
Sion

19
Angers region

20
'Tremeollo'

21
Camiliaco

22
Bordeaux

23
Probably Laon

24
'Castra'

25
Quentowic

26
Valence

27
Arles

28
Mouzon

29
Metz

30
Andernach

31
Sens

32
? Jaujac

33
Usson-du-Poitou

34
? Tours region

35
Javols

36
N. Gaul

37
Rodez area

38
blank

39
blank

40
blank

41
ingot

42
ingot

date when the coins can have come together and that of their burial.

The hoard was contained in a purse. This need not imply that coins were in use. All sorts of scrap gold, jewels, small ingots of gold or silver, and rings, might have been kept in a purse, a not unfamiliar item of the rich Germanic man's equipment.[52] The presence of blanks and ingots, on the other hand, might seem to suggest the minting of coin or provision for it. The weights of the three blanks, however (1.090, 1.380 and 1.462 gm), are not typically those of the coins of this series, which usually range from 1.25 and 1.35 gm. They were presumably then not thought of as awaiting striking, and there is certainly no indication that they are defaced coins, rubbed smooth for re-striking. They might, however, as Dr Kent suggests, be rejects even as blank flans, as not being within the acceptable weight-limits for minting, which were none the less used as a means of exchange on the basis of weight alone. The ingots are of a size from which the metal for such flans could be conveniently cut, but the three flans did not come from either of the ingots, since the analysis of the metal shows them to be of a different alloy. The blanks and ingots could have been included in the original consignment of coins, either as potential coins (i.e. raw material for striking more coins), or to make up a certain weight of gold. The blanks and ingots need not thus of themselves imply that coins were being struck locally in East Anglia. Indeed were it so, one would expect East Anglian issues to appear in the purse.

If the date of the burial is as early as AD 625–30, however, this period is one in which East Anglia was pagan, and before its contacts with the Christian Frankish kingdoms—contacts that soon became of some substance—matured. It is very unlikely that at this time coins were being struck, or were circulating, in East Anglia. It is also improbable that blanks and billets should have been added on the Continent to make up a certain weight of gold, when this could have been done by adding more of the coins which were struck and circulated there in plenty.

It seems to me that a suggestion by Professor Philip Grierson[53] bids fair to solve the problem of the coins, blanks and billets. It gives them a positive significance and seems to offer a satisfactory and exciting explanation of all the facts. Everything falls neatly into place.

Briefly, Professor Grierson noted the relatively miserly contents of the purse, in relation to the treasure as a whole. The forty coins scarcely add up in weight to a single minor piece of jewellery. This led him to the idea that what was significant about the coins to those who provided them for the purse was not so much their value as their number. This was brought up to 40 by the provision of three blanks. No other blanks are known in the corpus of Merovingian coinage,[54] except in the case of the mixed hoard of English and Frankish gold tremisses found at Crondall in Hampshire.[55] This hoard also had three blanks, which brought the number up to 100. Professor Grierson suggests that the hoard represented a free man's *wergild* or blood-price, which was 100 shillings in contemporary Kentish laws. Now 40 is (according to the latest calculation, p. 77 and footnote 39) the number of oarsmen that manned the ship. Professor Grierson has made the brilliant suggestion that the purpose of the coins was to pay the wages of the 40 oarsmen who were concerned in taking the ship to its destination in the after-life. The two billets would be the pay of the steersman. Their weight taken together (10.18 gm) is almost exactly eight times that of the average weight of the Sutton Hoo coins (1.27 gm).

This suggestion opens up many interesting new lines of thought and speculation. From the numismatic point of view it would reinforce the evidence, which must in the nature of the case be negative, that coins were not being struck or circulating in East Anglia at the time of the burial.

To summarize the position as to the evidence provided by the coins for the date of the burial, the most recent numismatic studies give a date of *c.* 625–30 at the latest for the coming together of these thirty-seven coins. This date can now be relied upon. In addition, the likelihood of time-lag between the coming together of the coins (probably in France, since these are a group of Merovingian coins which do not have the character of a merchant's hoard) and their interment on the occasion of a royal funeral in England, has to be borne in mind in estimating their date of deposition, that is to say, the date of the Sutton Hoo burial. The date now accepted however, is as Dr Kent has made clear, only a *terminus post quem* for the burial.

CHAPTER VII

Who was he?

This question, for whom the great Sutton Hoo ship and its contents were buried, has been discussed at length in other places.[56] It is hopeless to attempt to answer the question at all unless we can first accept that the burial is that of one of the kings of the East Angles in whose territory it lies. Fortunately it is virtually certain that it is, and this makes it worth persevering with the attempt to identify the person concerned, since we know the names and sequence of all the kings of East Anglia in the seventh century, and, either precisely or within very small margins, the years of their deaths. The factors which indicate that the burial is that of a king, and of no lesser person, and that it is not the burial of a foreigner, have also been gone into at length elsewhere.[57] Those indicating that it is a king's grave include its much greater richness as compared with all other known graves at the aristocratic or princely levels,[58] its close agreement with the contents of the few kings' graves that are known, particularly that of the Frankish King Childeric I (*d*. 481), and with the significant vestiges, meagre though these are, from the royal cremations in the great mounds at Old Uppsala, in the Uppland province of Sweden—a highly relevant parallel.[59] Other factors strongly suggestive of royalty are the presence of two unparalleled objects, the ceremonial stone crowned by a bronze stag, and the iron stand, which can it seems either most reasonably, or only, be interpreted as emblems of royal office (pp. 26–31). The unparalleled gold harness (purse, shoulder-clasps, buckles, sword fittings, strap mounts, etc.) also seems to have the character of an official outfit, regalia rather than personal ornaments.[60]

Once we are prepared to accept that the burial is that of an East Anglian king the decision as to which can only be determined by such evidence of date as the coins can offer, matched with the information that is to be gleaned from written sources, chiefly Bede, about the ruling members of the dynasty.

Two aspects of the burial, apart from its royalty, are relevant to the identification of the person for whom it was carried out. First, it has

EAST ANGLIAN KINGS

THE WUFFINGAS

(To save space, the descent through WODEN is shown horizontally. Those who came to the throne are shown in black type.)

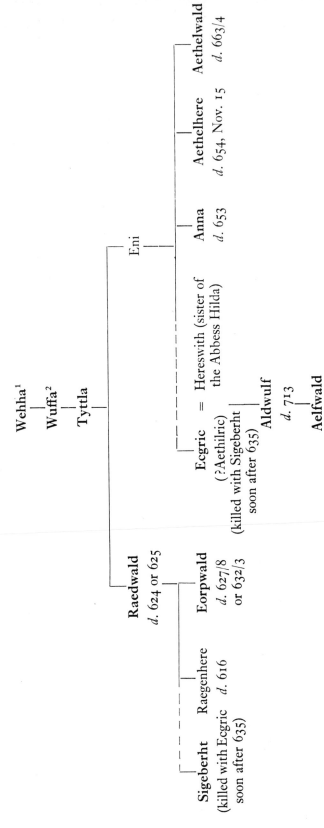

Frealaf—Woden—Caser—Tyttman—Trygil—Hrothmund—Hryp—Wilhelm—

Wehha[1]

Wuffa[2]

Tyttla

Eni

Raedwald *d.* 624 or 625

Anna *d.* 653

Aethelhere *d.* 654, Nov. 15

Aethelwald *d.* 663/4

Ecgric (?Aethilric) (killed with Sigeberht soon after 635) = Hereswith (sister of the Abbess Hilda)

Eorpwald *d.* 627/8 or 632/3

Sigeberht (killed with Ecgric soon after 635)

Raegenhere *d.* 616

Aldwulf *d.* 713

Aelfwald *d.* 749

[1] 'The first to rule over the East Angles in Britain', according to a gloss against his name in the *Historia Brittonum*.

[2] Hence members of the kingly family were called Wuffingas.

Note : In this table the chronology of Stenton and Poole is followed.

been claimed that this was a cenotaph, i.e. there was never a body in the burial-chamber, whether inhumed or cremated. Secondly, there are clear indications in the burial itself, if not that the man commemorated was himself a Christian, at least, that Christianity had made an impact on the royal court before the burial took place.

Thus we can say, without reference to the coins, that the signs of Christianity—the ten bowls chased with equal-armed crosses (*32, 77*), and the christening spoons (*33, 80*) with Saul and Paul on them, and their placing at what would be thought of as the dead man's shoulder, had a body been there (*7*); and the equal-armed crosses that form the basic design of the scabbard-bosses,[61] are so specific that no candidate could be considered for the burial before Raedwald; for Raedwald was the first of the East Anglian kings to be converted, although he subsequently relapsed, and the country remained heathen for some years after his death.[62]

If the numismatists' view (p. 87), favouring *c.* AD 625 as the latest date for the assembly of the coins found in the purse, accepted, Raedwald, whose death is placed in AD 624 or 625, is the ideal candidate. He was much the most powerful and successful king thrown up by the dynasty and, as Bretwalda or High King (the only East Anglian to achieve this position), had attained authority over the other Saxon kingdoms. His conversion in Kent, at Aethelberht's court, could easily explain the Christian objects, no doubt gifts, in the grave. His subsequent relapse could account for his burial in the pagan tradition in a burial ground with pagan associations,[63] and not, as became the rule immediately with converted royalty, in a church. Indeed, Raedwald's attempt to get the best of both worlds, by scandalously setting up altars to Christ and to the devil side by side might explain any mixture of Christian and pagan features in the burial. The pre-eminence of the burial seems to match perfectly the pre-eminence of Raedwald. The standard, if it can still be considered such (p. 27), and stone sceptre could well be symbols of his high office as Bretwalda, an office which on his death left the Wuffing family and passed to King Edwin of Northumbria.

If this is Raedwald's burial, however, we known of no reason why his body should not have been placed in it.

The identification with Raedwald, once a Christian but at least half-pagan at his death, might be compatible with the tenuous guess made at a possible, but somewhat freakish, explanation of the chemically inferred cremated bone source on the Anastasius dish. This is to say, in the case of Raedwald alone, the body might conceivably have been cremated, but the funeral portion, the ship and grave goods, left unburnt— a unique mixture of two fundamentally difference concepts, and, as already indicated against known practice. Cremation was not compatible at this period with the Christian burial, but the unique mixture of rites which the Sutton Hoo ship-burial, thus explained, would represent, might possibly reflect a unique pagan-Christian compromise such as Raedwald is known to have adopted.

The family tree of the Wuffingas, to which most East Anglian kings belonged, is given in a table on p. 94.[64] If we follow the dating which numismatists have now arrived at, giving outside limits for the actual burial of about AD 615–640, then the four kings Raedwald (d. 624 or 5), Eorpwald (d. c. 627 or 632), Sigeberht and Ecgric (both d. 635 or 6) would call to be considered.

Such a great burial seems quite unsuited to a Christian king, educated amongst the Merovingian Franks, who retired to a monastery and became a professed monk, and only emerged to be killed when brought out against his will to join Ecgric in leading the East Anglian army against an invasion by Penda of Mercia. This would seem to rule out Sigeberht. Ecgric, killed with Sigeberht, is a possibility; his successor and, it is suggested, brother Anna[64] would then have been the man who caused the monument to be constructed. We do not know whether Ecgric or Anna's brother Aethelhere were Christians or not, although the eleventh-century Life of St Botolph indicates that Aethelhere was.[65] Of Anna we know that he was a devout Christian, all of whose daughters became nuns, and three of them saints,[66] and that, according to an apparently reliable entry in the Ely chronicle, he was buried at Blythburgh, where his body was still venerated in the twelfth century. It is therefore unlikely that Anna would commemorate Ecgric in this pagan way. His younger brother Aethelwald (d. 663/4) was also a Christian, since he stood godfather to the Saxon king, Swithhelm, when the latter was baptized at Rendlesham between 655 and 664. Rendlesham is only a few miles from Sutton Hoo, and this event may be thought to imply the presence of a church there at the time.[67] These last kings are too late to consider, however.

As the christianization of East Anglia, and particularly of its royal family, progresses, it becomes increasingly difficult to allot the great burial in the pagan grave-field, for the practice of burying Christian kings in consecrated ground, in abbeys or churches, was introduced with St Augustine's mission to Kent, and seems to have been everywhere followed. Thus in East Anglia, the monk Sigeberht, if his body was recovered from the battlefield, was no doubt buried in a monastery, and Anna, as we have reason to think, was buried in the church at Blythburgh. It is this severance, especially in the case of royalty, from the old burial grounds, with their pagan associations, and burial instead in churches, rather than merely a provision of rich grave-goods, which makes it difficult to see the Sutton Hoo burial as the grave of a Christian king, and which makes Raedwald, a transitional figure, more pagan than

Christian in his known outlook, so suitable a candidate for this sumptuous burial.

The change-over to Christianity was a tolerant process, effected gradually, and in the period of transition abnormalities could occur. Thus while we could not accept the monument as the monk Sigeberht's grave, it could conceivably be accepted as his cenotaph. His burial in his own monastery would meet the Christian requirement; the bodiless public monument with its appropriate treasures would uphold the traditions of a proud dynasty and satisfy the instincts of a people still perhaps predominantly pagan. Again, Ecgric might, for all we know, have been pagan and yet had at his disposal a treasury containing Christian objects of gold and silver handed down from the days of Raedwald's half-hearted conversion, or the conversion of Raedwald's son Eorpwald at the instigation of Edwin of Northumbria, or from the Christian Sigeberht's days of power. Aethelhere would fit the cenotaph theory, for he was killed at the battle of Winwaed in Yorkshire, on 15 November 654, with all his following, and Bede records of this battle that 'many more were drowned in the flood waters in trying to escape, than were killed in the battle'.[68] Aethelhere's body in these conditions was very likely not recovered for burial. The numismatic evidence, however, must now be held to exclude both Aethelhere and his predecessor Anna.

With regard to the Cenotaph issue, the final study of chemical and other evidence from the burial suggests that a body may have been present after all, although this cannot be proved.

Enough has been said to show what the possibilities are of identifying the person for whom the Sutton Hoo ship-burial was arranged. It would be well worth making the identification, for this would enable us to tie the Sutton Hoo burial precisely to the year, or to two or three years. Such precision would be of the greatest value to archaeologists and historians. The evidence strongly favours Raedwald (*d.* 624/5) and no earlier king is possible. Ecgric (*d.* 635/6) however must also be considered a possibility, and thus Raedwald's son, Eorpwald (*d.* 627/8 or 632/3), cannot be excluded either.

CHAPTER VIII

The silver

General

The silver found in the Sutton Hoo ship seems to be a haphazard collection of pieces of different dates and from different sources. In this it stands in contrast to the gold jewellery, the bulk of which has every appearance of having been made in one workshop, perhaps even by one goldsmith.

All the silver objects seem to have been made in eastern Europe, Constantinople, or the Near East. The spoons were derived from models of the late classical period; the matching set of bowls were probably made in outlying provinces of the Byzantine Empire. With the other objects of foreign origin in the grave, they illustrate in a striking manner the far-flung connections of a seventh-century Anglo-Saxon royal house. Sufficient is not known about silver made in the provinces of the Byzantine Empire, however, to date any of the pieces (apart from the great dish) with certainty, or to say exactly where they were made.

Comparison with the fourth-century Roman silver treasure from Mildenhall[69] shows great differences in the workmanship and artistic quality seen in the latter Sutton Hoo vessels. This does not make their turning up in a Saxon grave on the opposite side of Europe from their place of origin any the less astonishing or diminish their great archaeological importance. It makes it likely, however, that, like the Red Sea cowrie shells and 'Coptic' bowls found in Saxon graves, some pieces found their way to England by trade.[70] They are not close enough to work done in the principal artistic centres, nor of sufficient merit in themselves, to be gifts from people of consequence, like, for example, the presents sent by popes to English kings and queens mentioned by Bede.[71] Yet the sixteen pieces of silver are one of the most remarkable features of the burial. Hardly another Germanic grave in Europe has produced so much as a single piece of antique silver with the exception of spoons and strainers and of the *phalerae* or horse-trappings from the rich burial at Ittenheim, in Bavaria.

The Anastasius Dish (49–51, 76)

Diameter, 28½ in. (72.4 cm). The delicate, rather fussy, minute ornament incised on the great dish (76) is characteristic of a late antique style that came into fashion before AD 400. Yet the dish is dated to the years AD 491–518, a hundred years later, by its control stamps (50, 51). The use of this earlier delicate style, the consistent employment of such microscopic and delicate ornament on such a vast dish, and the carelessness with which the design is drawn out, explain Professor Ernst Kitzinger's description of this dish as 'a very conservative work of a back-street artisan, clinging to old formulae'.[72] The unusually deep and heavy base ring and the extra band of ornament inserted between the central roundel and the decorated rim are features peculiar to this dish. It is also unique as the only demonstrably Byzantine object, apart from an occasional coin, to have been found in this extreme north-west corner of Europe. The association on one dish of four impressions from two different control stamps is peculiar to the reign of Anastasius I, and occurs on all five silver vessels stamped in his reign.

The Fluted Bowl with Classical Head (53, 82)

This bowl is 15½–16 in. (39.4–40.6 cm) in diameter, and the second largest of the silver pieces. It is clearly not of the same school or style as the Anastasius dish. Although obviously Mediterranean in background, its date and place of origin are not easily determined. The flutings are shallow and weak; the female profile head, a deliberate but laboured reaching back to the classical manner, is stiff and crude, disfigured by the central compass mark and rather unhappily out of equilibrium in its roundel (82). The two drop-handles lack the grace and movement of the elegant swan's neck handles of the Mildenhall fluted bowl, with which it should be compared.[73] Altogether, although it is beaten from a great weight of solid silver, and the hair nicely contrived, it has no great claim to either artistic or technical merit.

The Set of Ten Silver Bowls (32, 77)

Only seven of these are fit for exhibition.[74] They are shallow, light, circular bowls, varying in diameter between 8.1 and 9.1 in. (20.5–23.3 cm), without foot or rim and with only a slight internal beading at the rim. Each is decorated with an equal-armed cross inscribed into the inside of the bowl. A chased star motive is repeated along the arms of the cross, and in the centre is a circular ornament which varies in every other bowl. The designs are shown in 77. Bowls 1–8 comprise four pairs, but the designs of 9 and 10 differ. These vessels are paralleled in treasures like the Lampsacus treasure,[75] that have a specifically Christian character, and probably themselves have Christian significance. They can hardly have been made much before AD 600.

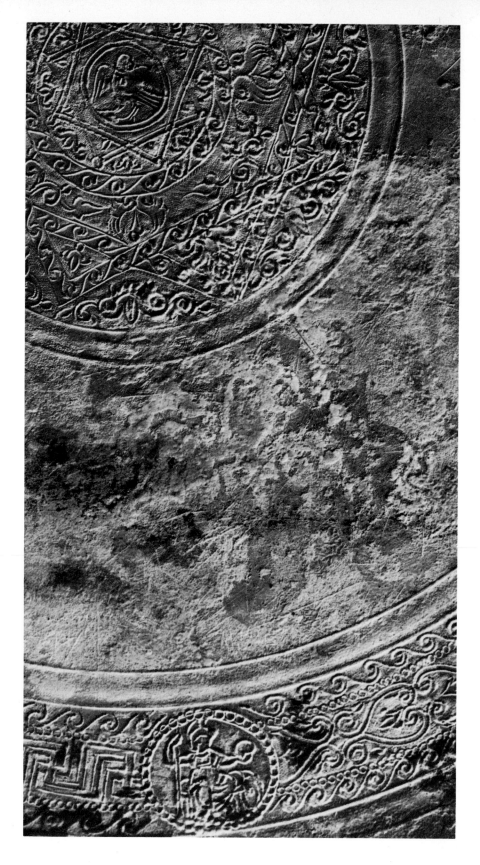

76 The Anastasius dish:
detail of the ornament.
(Scale, 4/3)

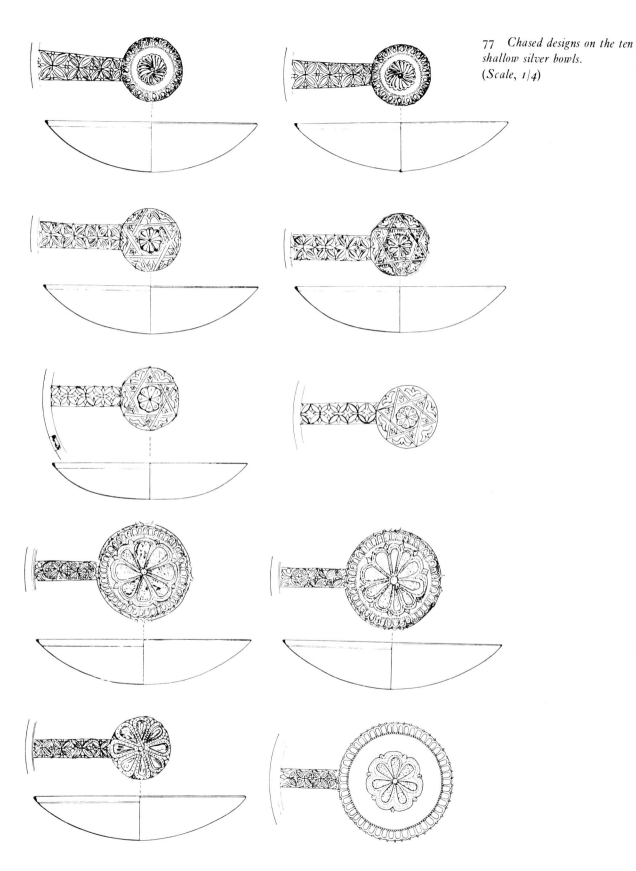

77 *Chased designs on the ten shallow silver bowls.*
(*Scale, 1/4*)

The Spoons (33)

These are of a well-known late-classical type. They are 10 in. (25.4 cm) in length and have solid, vertically set discs at the junction of bowl and stem, and moulded handles. It has been suggested that sets of spoons of this type were made to sell as mementoes at shrines connected with the cult of the twelve apostles. The Sutton Hoo spoons, however, have been regarded as a pair, since there are two of them in the burial, identical in form (though not in condition) and bearing the complementary names, Saul and Paul (Saulos and Paulos). The allusion to St Paul is clear, and as they occur together, as a pair, a specific allusion to his conversion seems intended. If so, the spoons may fairly be regarded as having been conceived as a baptismal present for a convert (such as Raedwald was); not an infant to be baptized, but rather an adult, changing, like St Paul, from the pagan to the Christian state.

It has been said that the name Saul, referring to the Saint's pagan life and his days as a persecutor of Christians, would not appear on a spoon intended for liturgical use, that is, for use during the celebration of the Mass, or other sacraments of the Church; this is no doubt so, and it is a fact that, amongst the very many late-antique or Byzantine spoons that survive, none, apart from the unique instance at Sutton Hoo, so far as is known, bears the name Saul. There is, however, no suggestion that these spoons, even bearing Christian inscriptions or symbols, were intended for liturgical use. The theory that inscribed spoons were made as souvenirs for pilgrims to holy places has been referred to above. They may have been given as presents, and been in secular use, like the Apostle spoons of more modern times. The names Saul and Paul in association on two spoons, as we have them at Sutton Hoo, would suggest that such pairs were sometimes made as christening presents.

However, an American scholar has recently argued that the spoons at Sutton Hoo both bear the name Paul (Paulus).[76] It will be seen that

78 *The names Saul and Paul as inscribed in Greek on the two silver spoon handles. (Scale, 1/1)*

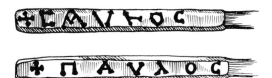

on one (*78b*) the name is engraved in evenly spaced, orthodox letters of regular size, whereas on the other (*78a*) it is less skilfully done. The inscription is less well spaced out, the letters vary in size, the L (*lambda*) is written backwards and set obliquely, a different type of A is used, the arms of the V do not meet, the O is a poor effort compared with the true circle seen in *78b*. This inscription is clearly by a different hand, less skilled and less literate than that of *78b*. It could be that the

first letter, S (*sigma*), is really a P (*pi*) misplaced (as though the engraver began the inscription as if it were to be read downwards, rather than along). Such spoons may have been manufactured without inscriptions, which were added locally, as required, and, in this instance, by craftsmen of unequal capacity.

If this were so, i.e. that both spoons bear the name Paulos, the spoons would not need to be seen as a pair, or as having reference to conversion. None the less it remains true that the names can be read as Saulos and Paulos, as indeed they have been, and the allusion to conversion, seen in the juxtaposition of the spoons, may well have been deliberate, intended by those who gave or possessed the spoons, even though originally the engravers may have intended to write the name Paul in both instances. Indeed it would be curious if a grave contained a pair of spoons both with the name Paul. The case for a deliberate Christian reference is weakened by Dr Kaske's acute observations, but not necessarily destroyed.

Opposite: 80 *The gold purse-lid, restored; the mounts are decorated with garnets and millefiori glass. (Scale, 1/1)*

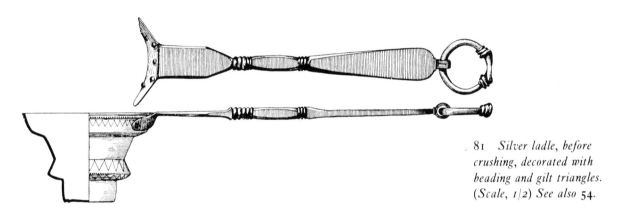

81 *Silver ladle, before crushing, decorated with beading and gilt triangles. (Scale, 1/2) See also* 54.

Numerous spoons from early Christian treasures are normally exhibited with the Byzantine and early Christian objects, and spoons inscribed with Christian symbols are to be seen in the Mildenhall treasure in the Roman Britain Room.

Other Silver Pieces

These are a plain silver bowl, $3\frac{1}{2}$ in. (8.9 cm) in diameter, with a foot-ring (*54*) and a silver ladle (*54, 81*) 2 in. (5.1 cm) high, with a stout handle ending in a terminal ring through which passes a silver wire loop. This ladle has delicate beading round its rim and the wide carinated moulding which appears lower down on its body angle, and in addition a frieze of gilded triangles under the rim and a double frieze of rather larger triangles, also gilded, on both faces of the carinated moulding. The ladle-cup was found pinched onto the base-ring of the Anastasius

82   *Fluted silver bowl: detail of the classical female head and surrounding zone of ornament. (Enlarged) See also 53.*

dish.[77] The photograph (*54*) shows how forcibly it was driven in, a circumstance which provides additional evidence for the violent collapse of the burial chamber.

CHAPTER IX

The jewellery

General

The purse-lid (*80*) consists of an outer frame enclosing seven decorative plaques and four circular studs. Outside the frame, at the bottom, is a detachable sliding catch. All these are of gold, and the purse contained gold coins and billets (*75*). The sword has a gold pommel, gold-mounted guards or quillons, and two small gold filigree mounts on the grip; and the scabbard has two gold bosses. Two gold truncated pyramids are also connected with the sword (*18*). In addition to these fittings of the purse and sword, there are no less than twenty other individual gold pieces. These are buckles, hinges, clasps, ornamental studs and mounts, and strap-mounts or distributors, and strap-ends, that held together and adorned the belt, baldric and outer harness of a royal apparel (see note 88). Such a wealth of gold has never before been found or even approached in any Anglo-Saxon grave.

All the gold pieces except the great belt-buckle (*79*) and one or two minor items (*18, 41, 87*) are jewelled with garnets. Over 4000 individually cut garnets are used in all the Sutton Hoo jewellery. The great majority of these are backed by patterned gold-foil and fitted into gold cells built up on a base-plate, the base-plate being part of the body of the object thus decorated. This is the cloisonné technique already familiar in the well-known garnet-encrusted gold jewels of the period made in Kent.[78] In the pair of gold clasps and the purse-lid (*39, 73, 80*), however, the goldsmith has developed the cloisonné technique in a highly original way. In the single plaque on the purse-lid (top centre) and the two outer plaques below (the man between beasts) and in the interlace borders around the rectangular panels on the clasps (*73, 85*) the garnets in parts of the design have the appearance of being sunk into solid metal.[79] The plain fields between and around these garnet elements in the design, however, are in reality cells, just like those which carry the garnets, often of the most irregular shapes, with thick gold lids brazed over their tops. This has been done so skilfully and solidly that, except here and there, no outward trace of the cloison underneath remains.

The most original and spectacular of the pieces—the purse-lid, curved clasps and pyramids (see p. 113 below)—are decorated with inset chequers of blue and white, or red and white *millefiori* glass, in addition to their garnet decoration. *Millefiori* appear on late Romano-British brooches, in Migration Period beads of Rhenish or Mediterranean manufacture, and on the escutcheons of some of the Celtic hanging-bowls found in Saxon graves.[80] At Sutton Hoo, *millefiori* appear for the first time in Germanic jewellery, and at the highest level, in the garnet-encrusted gold jewels that are the richest relics of the pagan Saxons, and in the making of which Saxon goldsmiths exerted their highest skill.

The Great Buckle (79)

The finest piece artistically amongst the Sutton Hoo jewellery is probably the great belt-buckle of solid gold, 5.2 in. (13.2 cm) long. In sheer weight of metal, $14\frac{5}{8}$ oz (414.62 gm), it outclasses any other Anglo-Saxon ornament known to us. The front of the buckle is decorated all over with flat interlacing animal patterns, the design picked out with tiny circles and (in the central element of the design) with lines and dots of inlaid niello. Three large plain bosses, surrounded by beaded collars, connect with sliding catches on the back plate, which opens about a hinge. To either side of the two upper bosses (79), powerful birds' heads in profile thrust downwards. Below them, half-way down the buckle, two animal heads at the edges of the buckle bite inwards across the inter-lace. To either side of the lower boss are two more animal heads, this time with open mouths, between which, across the end of the buckle, crouches, upside down, a little biting beast, very like that on a shield mount from Caenby, Lincs. (normally exhibited), and related to others in Anglo-Saxon art (*83*). The central interlace-element is made up of two snakes which end above the lower boss in outward-biting heads. The circular plate at the base of the buckle-tongue, which acts as a stop for the tongue, bears an admirably designed and compact animal inter-lace that is also closely paralleled on the Caenby shield-mounts. The panels on the buckle-loop, to either side of the tongue, have a zoo-morphic interlace with a biting head and tail; its intricately knotted un-tidiness, judged by later Saxon work, may be said to have a charac-teristically Anglian rhythm, but it is most closely paralleled on mounts found in boat-grave no. I at Vendel, in Uppland, Sweden.[81] The great buckle represents a different artistic tradition and a different taste from the gay polychrome jewellery heavily ornamented with garnets and coloured glass. It is also of a paler gold, with some 13 per cent of silver in the alloy, as against some 2 per cent in the other pieces. It seems without doubt to have been made in England, yet the style of its main interlace is strikingly like that of the ornaments found in the Swed-ish boat-graves. In fact, the buckle would not, in point of style, seem unduly out of place amongst material from the earliest boat-graves in the Vendel cemetery, although the buckle-type is unknown in Sweden.

(a) Sutton Hoo great gold buckle.

(b) Caenby, Lincs., shield mount.

(c) Crundale Down, Kent, sword pommel.

(d) Book of Durrow.

83 *The biting beast on the toe of the great belt-buckle and some of its relations. (b), (c) and (d) in their original compositions are all biting either their own limbs or the back of another creature. All show pear-shaped stylization of the hips. In most cases the treatment of the feet is similar. (c), (d), and (f) show collars at the ankles. (e) also from the Sutton Hoo gold buckle, shows the pair of parallel lines crossing the body from the front hip, seen more conspicuously in (a).*

(e) Sutton Hoo great gold buckle.

(f) Sutton Hoo, maplewood drinking vessel.

(g) Sutton Hoo purse-lid.

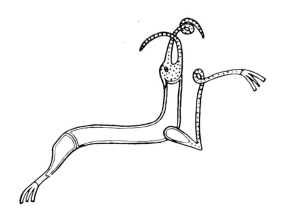

(h) Book of Durrow.

The Purse-lid (80)

The purse-lid is the most gorgeous of the finds. The gold outer frame, 7½ in. (19.05 cm) long, is jewelled with bars and panels of garnet and *millefiori* glass, and enriched with filigree bindings.[82] The material of the lid, in which the ornamental plaques and studs were sunk, was probably bone or ivory.[83] The lid hinges at the top on three gold plates, which were riveted to leather straps depending from a belt. At the bottom of the lid a projecting gold tongue engages with a simple and efficient sliding catch. The purse itself was probably a pouch-like bag hanging below the lid, the sliding catch being permanently attached to the mouth of the bag. The purse contained thirty-seven gold coins, all minted on the Continent (see Chapter VI and *74*) three blank flans and two plain gold billets (*75*).

The jewelled plaques (*80*) fall into three pairs, with one double plaque. The hexagonal pair at the top on either side of the double plaque are notable for the intricacy and delicacy of the cloisonné work. The outer pair of plaques below show a man standing spreadeagled between two rampant animals. This was at first thought to be a version of the 'Daniel in the Lion's Den' subject familiar on Frankish buckles, some of which bear the inscription *Daniel Profeta*. In the Frankish versions, however, the lions usually (though not always),[84] like St Menas' camels on Coptic pilgrims' flasks, have their heads down and their tails up in the air. There is a Scandinavian design very close indeed to that on the purse, however, which may possibly have an Eastern origin altogether different from that of the design on the Frankish buckles, or else is a native evolution in

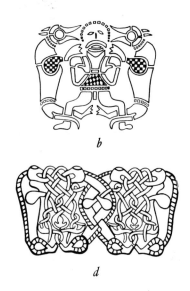

84 *Man and animals motif: (a) from Torslunda; (b) from the Sutton Hoo purse-lid. (Scales, 1/1) Linked pairs of confronted animals with interlacing limbs: (c) from the shield-boss; (d) from the purse-lid. (Scales, (c) approximately 2/3; (d) 1/1)*

a

b

c

d

Scandinavia. In this the animals stand erect on their hind legs, as in the Sutton Hoo plaques. The best example of this Scandinavian theme is a very well-known stamp for embossing bronze plates for decorating helmets, from Björnhovda, Torslunda, on Öland, Sweden, (84a).[85] It also occurs on the helmet, recently published in detail, from boat-grave VII at Valsgärde, in Uppland. The 'man and monster' plaques on the Sutton Hoo purse seem to be a further instance of the Swedish connection with Sutton Hoo, discussed below.[86] The two central plaques in the lower ornamental register represent a bird of prey swooping on a duck. The eyes of both birds are interesting. They are circular garnets, in which are engraved circles filled with blue glass. The double plaque (top centre) has symmetrical pairs of animals, the pairs interlocked back to back, with their fluent limbs, executed in cut garnets, interlacing against plain gold grounds (84d), it is a fine example of the new lidded-cloison technique, and a wonderful piece of virtuosity. The purse as a whole forms the most attractive and sumptuous trapping ever found in a Teutonic grave.

The Shoulder-clasps (39, 73)

These are amongst the most remarkable objects in the find. In type, shape and decoration they are unique. The rectangular panels, filled with regular lines of cells in step-pattern cloisonné and framed by broad borders of animal interlace, show an all-over carpet-like design that seems to be of great art-historical importance, since it foreshadows in striking and specific fashion a decorated page in the Book of Durrow, a Hiberno-Saxon[87] illuminated manuscript produced in Northumbria perhaps half a century later than the date of the manufacture of these clasps. For the first time a 'carpet-pattern' design, such as later becomes typical of the decorative pages of rich gospel books like those of Lindisfarne and Kells, has appeared in a pagan Anglo-Saxon context. The interlace patterns in the borders of the clasps (85) are additional instances of the covered-cloison or lidded-cloison technique, with its champlevé effect. Coloured *millefiori* glass is liberally used in the panels and at the ends of the clasps.

The clasps hinge centrally about long thick gold pins that end in animal heads encrusted with annular filigree, and originally had tiny garnet eyes. The pins are attached to the clasps by delicate gold chains, and can be withdrawn, when the clasps fall apart (39). On the backs are numerous strong gold staples, by which the clasps were evidently sewn on to cloth or leather. They were probably worn on the shoulders, to which their curvature and weight is suited, affixed to the front and back of a two-piece garment, surcoat or cuirass, assembled on the body by joining the halves of the clasps, which would be permanently sewn onto the two distinct halves of the garment. It has recently been suggested that ultimately they copied the hinged shoulder-fittings of the leather or metal cuirass of Roman parade-armour, of high-ranking commanders and as seen on Imperial effigies until the Byzantine era.[88]

Perhaps the most remarkable thing about these clasps is the design of two intersecting boars with tusks and crested backs that appears

85 *Animal interlaced themes from the borders round the cloisonné panels of the shoulder-clasps. (Scale, 1/1)*

86 *Design of two intersecting boars from the ends of the shoulder-clasps. (Scale, 1/1)*

at either end of each clasp (*86*). The boar is a familiar subject in Celtic art, but less common in pagan Saxon art.[89] The crested spines on the animals and their lowered heads forcibly suggests a comparison with the late Saxon (eleventh century) boar on a tympanum at St Nicholas Church, Ipswich. The bodies and haunches of these boars are made up of large plate-garnets. This use of such unprecedented expanses of garnet, seen also in the bodies of the birds and animals in the purse-lid plaques, is another distinctive characteristic of the work of the Sutton Hoo master, and results from his objective, the depicting in this medium of naturalistic and narrative themes, in contrast to the usual small-scale abstract patterns of cells.

The interstices of the pattern between the boars' heads and legs are filled with snake or animal figures in filigree. Filigree decoration is very common in the cloisonné jewellery of Kent,[90] and its relative rarity at Sutton Hoo, and the use instead of continuous all-over spreads of garnet and *millefiori* glass is yet another distinctive characteristic of the new school.

The Sword (*18, 37*)

The sword was buried in its scabbard, and blade and scabbard are now inseparably rusted into one solid mass. It is impossible to recover full details of either, though certain features are apparent. There was probably leather next to the blade, and a wooden outer sheath, which in turn was bound in places with cloth. Such seems, provisionally, to have been the construction of the scabbard. There seems to have been a groove running down it for some four inches from the lower guard, and to either side of this two hemispherical jewelled bosses (*18*) were fixed (*37*). The overall length of the sword in its present state is 2 ft 9½ in. (85 cm), the blade about 28 in. (71 cm): it is shorter than the majority of Anglo-Saxon swords. Radiography reveals that the blade is finely forged in the pattern-welding technique, with a multiple chevron pattern.[91]

The pommel is of gold, and its convex and concave surfaces are set with a perfect assembly of congruently curved garnets. A very similar jewelled gold pommel has been found in Sweden,[92] and the cloisonné on other Swedish pommels seems to be related to Sutton Hoo work.[93] On the hilt are two gold filigree mounts. The guard or quillon mounts are also of gold. The scabbard-bosses are decorated with a cross in the centre of a unique petal-like design, set up in wedge-shaped slices of garnet with corresponding wedge-shaped covered cells between them. A double row of minute serrated garnets runs round the edges of the bosses. No other English-found sword has scabbard-bosses or buttons, but scabbard-bosses, similarly placed and of similar size, appear on swords carried by warrior-figures on Swedish helmets from the Vendel sites.

The Pyramids (18)

These small jewels are of miraculous workmanship, and must be among the most remarkable objects in Teutonic archaeology. To quote Sir Thomas Kendrick, 'it can be doubted if any ancient lapidary in the whole of the Teutonic world has produced jewels that rival these tiny pieces in the delicacy of the stone-cutting and in the accurate elegance of the assembled whole'.[94] The upper edges and angles of the pyramids are cut in solid garnet, and the tops each enclose a dainty square of *millefiori* glass. The backs are slotted, and as they were found one on either side of the sword, we can assume that they decorated the sword-knot, or perhaps were mounted on a narrow strap that passed through the scabbard bosses.[95]

The Other Pieces

The other jewels, less spectacular, are nevertheless of great importance. Two flat mounts show a rendering of the simple twist in cloisonné garnets (40). Interlace patterns represented thus are excessively rare, and only two other Teutonic jewels are known on which this piece of technical virtuosity is attempted with a similar delicacy of treatment, the remains of a once splendid brooch of what we must now call the 'Sutton Hoo' school, found at Faversham, Kent, now in the British Museum, and a fragment of a gold cloisonné pyramid from one of the great mounds containing cremations at Gamla Uppsala, Sweden.[96] Two other flat mounts (40) show the use of a mushroom-shaped cell (88, d, e, f) which occurs only on a few other Saxon gold jewels that we may now have to attribute to the workshop of the Sutton Hoo master. The mushroom-cell in one form or another appears on practically every one of the Sutton Hoo mounts and buckles (*40, 41*), and may be regarded as the characteristic theme of the Sutton Hoo master and his workshop.

A T-shaped mount (strap distributor) hinges ingeniously in two planes, the hinges, as in all the moving parts of these gold jewels, operating with perfect smoothness after thirteen hundred years in the ground. Even the working part of the hinge is inset with garnets. A similar decorative exuberance is shown in the unique dummy buckle (*40*) with an imitation tongue cut away across the loop. In this garnets are inset all round the buckle loop. A minute animal cut out of a curve of gold

87 (a)*Animal figure in curved gold foil with gold attachment pins at the back;* (b) *fluted gold strip with animal head;* (c) *animals engraved on small gold foil triangle (Scales, 1/1)*

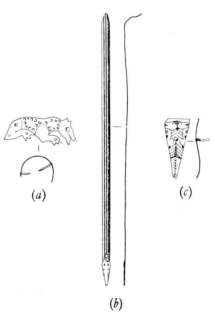

(a)

(b)

(c)

foil, with pins at the back for attachment (*41, 87a*) is also worthy of note.

The remaining gold objects are all illustrated (*40, 41*). One was found lying obliquely across the scabbard, and one near the purse. The ring-headed strip which lay on the scabbard is enriched with filigree work, in addition to its four *cabochon* or convex garnets. The diameter of the ring at its top is the same as that of the gold foil animal (*41, 87a*), when the latter is slightly compressed into a circle, and they were probably mounted on the same object, which, from the high distribution of phosphate on the scabbard where they lay, was probably a bone or ivory wand. All the individual cell-types used in the Sutton Hoo jewellery (*88*), and some of the characteristic cell-combinations or themes (*89*) are shown. The naturalistic or semi-naturalistic representations achieved in the cloisonné medium (*90*) are not attempted in this manner or at this level of accomplishment and sophistication in any other surviving cloisonné work of the period.[97]

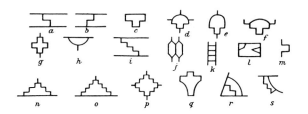

88   *Basic cell-shapes used in the Sutton Hoo jewellery. (Scale, 1/1)*

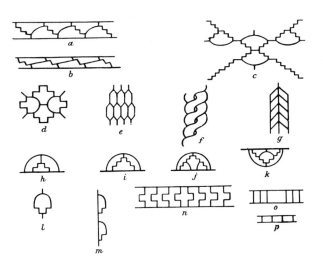

89   *Geometric patterns occurring in the Sutton Hoo jewellery, built up from the basic cell-shapes. See also 88. (Scale, 1/1)*

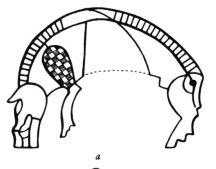

90   *Figural or naturalistic themes in the Sutton Hoo jewellery. (a) from the shoulder-clasps; (b) the curved gold-foil animal; (c–g) from the purse-lid. (Scales, 1/1)*

CHAPTER X

The Swedish connection

Of very special significance at Sutton Hoo is the connection it reveals with Sweden (*91*).[98]

Briefly, the sword with the pommel (but not the scabbard or scabbard-bosses, or the pyramids from the sword-knot); the shield with its 'sword-ring', the helmet and possibly other items in the burial were all probably either made in Sweden itself or by armourers, fresh from Sweden, working in Suffolk, exclusively in their traditional manner and using Swedish dies, moulds and other equipment.[99]

Such pieces appearing in Suffolk by themselves could, of course, be simply spoils of war or gifts, and need imply no deeper link. However, we also find that the fabulous great gold buckle (not a Swedish piece, but locally made) is decorated in what seems to be unmistakably Swedish style. The Swedish aspect of its interlace was indeed commented upon by Sir Thomas Kendrick while the buckle was still in the ground. Furthermore, the naturalistic subjects on the purse-lid seems to demonstrate the incursion of the distinctive Swedish figural art of the Vendel period (the art, in particular, of the helmets) into the locally made regalia, or at least into its most sumptuous piece. The man-between-beasts scene in spite of the obvious differences is intimately related to the similar scene depicted on one of the well-known bronze dies from Torslunda, Öland (used for stamping foil sheeting for application to helmets). Another instance, and one especially striking, since it refers to a Swedish-style piece in the Sutton Hoo grave, is the central double-plaque at the top of the purse-lid. This design, otherwise unique, seems to be a version—a translation into the more stylized, less naturalistic medium of jewellery—of the theme of pairs of erect and interlocked horses on the flange of the shield boss (*21, 84c*).

Thus the Swedish element appears, archaeologically, as a powerful leaven, in a milieu which is that of the East Anglian court; and it is to be noted that the most intimate connections of all with Swedish material are with certain of the cremated vestiges recovered from the Swedish royal mounds at Old Uppsala.

Opposite:

91 Outline map of north-west Europe, showing the relationship of Scandinavian sites mentioned to East Anglia.

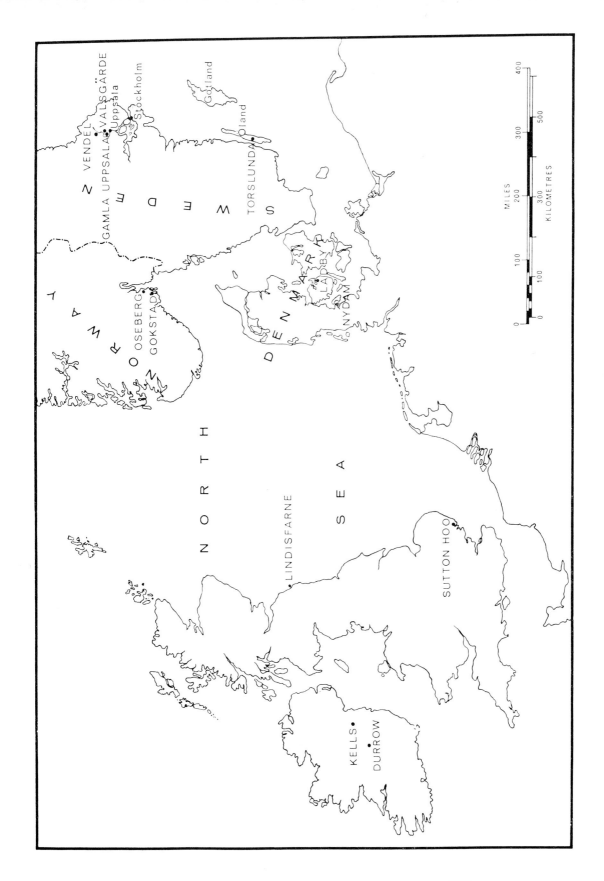

GOTLAND

VENDEL
VALSGÄRDE
GAMLA UPPSALA
Uppsala
Stockholm

S W E D E N

TORSLUNDA
Öland

N O R W A Y

OSEBERG
GOKSTAD

D E N M A R K

LADBY
NYDAM

MILES
KILOMETRES

400
300
200
100
0

500
300
100
0

N O R T H

S E A

LINDISFARNE

SUTTON HOO

KELLS
DURROW

117

To this unparalleled combination of factors, concentrated in a single grave, we add that at this early date—in the seventh century—the custom of elaborately furnished boat-inhumation, which becomes widespread later, in the Viking age, as does boat-cremation, is at present found only in two places in Europe, the Uppland province of Sweden and south-east Suffolk (the two boat-inhumations at Sutton Hoo and the one at Snape (p. 80).[100] These two areas share, apparently uniquely at this time, a burial-ritual of a highly distinctive kind.

The most plausible explanation of the hard fact of the Swedish connection seen at Sutton Hoo at the royal level would seem to be that it is dynastic. The possible antiquity of some of the Swedish pieces at Sutton Hoo, especially the helmet, suggests that the connection goes back into a period earlier than the burial. The most likely explanation seems to be that the dynasty of the Wuffingas was Swedish in its origin, and that probably Wehha, said to be the first of the family to rule over the Angles in Britain, was a Swede.

However, the names in the genealogy of the Wuffingas (p. 94) do not seem to have any parallels or analogues amongst those of the royal house of the Svear, the people from whose territory, to the north of the Mälar lake, the most striking archaeological parallels come, some of whose kings are buried in the great mounds at Old Uppsala. The names of the East Anglian royal genealogy seem to find their affinities, on the contrary, amongst those of the royal house of the Geats,[101] the traditional enemies of the Swedes, who occupied the areas of central Sweden, south of lakes Vännen and Vätten, in the territories now known as Västergotland and Östergotland. Beowulf, we may recall, was a Geat.

The picture at the Scandinavian end is thus not wholly clear, and it may at any time be modified by fresh archaeological discoveries. Rich boat-graves of the Vendel age may come to light in other parts of Sweden.[102] The specific, direct, east-Scandinavian link with the Vendel culture of Sweden, however, transcending the parallels and similarities that are common to many parts of western Europe, from north Italy to Kent and Sweden, in what is known to archaeologists as the 'Style II' area, seems quite clearly established.

Some of our continental colleagues may not be convinced of this direct link, though it has the powerful support of Sune Lindqvist, the former Professor of Northern Archaeology in Uppsala.[103] But those who know best the plentiful material of Anglo-Saxon archaeology are aware of the extent to which these elements stand out as something apart from their background, consanguineous perhaps, but without Anglo-Saxon roots. It is fascinating to see that as long ago as 1911, Reginald Smith, who knew the English material so well, suggested that two decorated bronze plates in the Bury St Edmunds Museum (dies for stamping patterns in foil) were brought over by a Swedish settler.[104]

A connection of this radical nature at the royal level could explain much that is distinctive about the archaeology both of the East Angles and of the Vendel culture in Sweden. The all-over style of the locally made cloisonné jewellery at Sutton Hoo, for example, so different from that of Kent, may derive from the Swedish workshops which, we believe, produced the Sutton Hoo sword-pommel and several close parallels to it from Swedish sites.

For students of Old English literature, a direct Scandinavian royal link of the sixth and seventh centuries must be of the greatest interest in connection with the problem of the transmission of the substance of *Beowulf*, its Scandinavian characters and setting, to its Anglo-Saxon milieu, and, indeed, with its creation here. In addition, the ship-burial itself and the objects in it, in many striking ways support and illuminate the *Beowulf* text. One authority, the late C. L. Wrenn, has gone so far as to call the discovery of the Sutton Hoo ship-burial 'perhaps the most important happening in Beowulf studies since the Icelander, Jón Grímer Thorkelin, made his transcriptions of the Beowulf MS and from them published the first edition of the poem.[105]

CHAPTER XI

Conclusions

The full significance of this great discovery will only be revealed with time, as other discoveries bearing on it are made in England and on the Continent, and when the grave-field in which it is set has been fully explored. The final publication of the excavation, the ship and the grave-goods will bring into print a wealth of additional detail. Some assessment, however, of the historical importance of the burial can and should be offered now.

The Sutton Hoo ship-burial reveals for the first time the material culture of the pagan Anglo-Saxons at the royal level. The culture it represents is that of the pagan era even if, by the year of the burial, Christianity may have become to some degree established. Hitherto we have judged the Anglo-Saxon attainment in their pagan period, so far as material culture is concerned, almost wholly by the contents of graves of second or third rank. Yet it is, of course, at the top level, that of the royal courts, that new influences are first entertained, that contacts with foreign lands and courts are most extensive and fertile. At this level also wealth was concentrated, the richest materials and the best craftsmanship met, and patronage was at its most imaginative and discriminating. Hence the sudden enlargement of horizons which the Sutton Hoo burial, our first royal grave, has brought, and its value as a key to movements in the arts and to historical development in the middle of a crucial century in English history.

In recent years we have gained new insight into the environment of a pagan seventh-century Anglo-Saxon court, in terms of architecture, from Dr Hope-Taylor's excavation of the Northumbrian royal seat at Yeavering, in the Cheviots, in the far north, beyond the Roman wall. Yeavering and Sutton Hoo together shed a new light both on the culture achieved in these early Anglo-Saxon kingdoms, and on the manner of courtly life, which before had to be inferred in general terms chiefly from *Beowulf* and other literary sources, but which now receives concrete illustration.

East Anglia, though it had its moment of political greatness under Raedwald, was by no means the richest or strongest of the early Anglo-Saxon kingdoms. We may safely infer that equal or greater splendours than those reflected at Sutton Hoo graced the courts of Northumbria, Mercia, Wessex and Kent, though we may doubt whether the workmanship at Sutton Hoo was anywhere surpassed in quality or interest. So it is that not only in East Anglia, but throughout Anglo-Saxondom our concept of the pagan Saxon achievement is lifted. We should also remember that what was buried at Sutton Hoo represents only a fraction of the riches that the royal treasury must have held, the part which might be written off on such an occasion; commensurate with the status of the dead man, yet only his portion.

The Sutton Hoo discoveries, particularly the jewellery, but also the native animal ornament and figural themes—birds, animals and men naturalistically conceived (90)—and the very wide range of stimulating foreign material seen to be present, precisely reverse the depressing picture previously drawn by the highest authority of the trend of pagan Saxon art in the middle of the century. Sir Thomas Kendrick wrote in 1938, with the Sutton Hoo treasure still concealed by the Suffolk turf, in relation to Anglo-Saxon art north of the Thames in the mid-seventh century, 'design still has considerable cunning, but lacks the authentic stamp of original barbaric vigour, and it would only be with very great reluctance that I should suggest we have in this Anglian development the source of that new and important flowering of the barbaric style that we soon encounter in the arts of Christian England'.[106] But the native antiquities as distinct from the imported silver and other objects, disinterred at Sutton Hoo a bare year after this view was expressed, reveal a completely unexpected school of art, and a supreme one. It is pagan Saxon art in its final flower, overloaded, but not decadent. The gold jewellery is brimming with novel and daring ideas. It shows an overflowing exuberance and displays the highest level of craftsmanship, excelling anything known in this medium from the rest of Europe in its era. We see now for the first time that in the earlier part of the seventh century the supremacy in material culture of Kent, by far the richest of the early Saxon kingdoms, might be challenged and even surpassed in East Anglia.

It is also clear that this East Anglian achievement is not just a development from Kentish exemplars. No doubt the gold jewellery has to some extent a Kentish ancestry, for gold jewels ornamented with cloisonné garnets and coloured glass and fine filigree work were long established in Kent. But the Sutton Hoo jewellery, with its all-over cloisonné style and use of glass *millefiori* and figural themes, differs greatly from the Kentish. The cloisonné technique is handled by the master-goldsmith in wholly un-Kentish ways. Many of the shapes and types of mount and buckle are unparalleled in Kent. The grave is full of unfamiliar objects. Clearly elements quite other than Kentish ones are present. There are those which imply a strong Swedish connection, and with these Kentish, British (i.e. Celtic), Frankish, and local Anglian elements seem to be combined in ways not previously seen to create a distinctive new local art and archaeology.[107]

This final flowering of pagan art does not fade with the establishment of Christianity. Why should it, when new opportunities and a vast new field of patronage were opening? It has already been noted that the rectangular panels on the hinged clasps, filled with regular spreads of geometric cells and framed by interlace (*73*, *85*), foreshadow the illuminated pages of later Christian manuscripts. The taste for carpet-like spreads of all-over ornament is also characteristic of both these panels and the later illuminated pages. This florid, all-over, heavily charged style is not confined to the clasps at Sutton Hoo. It is characteristic of the jewellery as a whole. Moreover, it is difficult to repress the feeling that the standard of perfection set by the Sutton Hoo master-goldsmith, the infinite pains taken, for instance, in the minute cloisonné work on the pair of hexagonal plaques on the purse-lid (*79*), reveal the spirit that is expressed in the work of the indefatigable and meticulous Northumbrian illuminators. The final phase of pagan Saxon art is seen to be its most vital; and it certainly made greater contributions than has hitherto been thought possible to the Northumbrian Renaissance and the development of Hiberno-Saxon art.[108]

In this connection, the three Celtic hanging-bowls have a special interest. Such bowls, and stray escutcheons from bowls, are not uncommon in Saxon graves, the bowls being often crudely patched and repaired. They are, broadly speaking, fossils, exotic things reft from their original context, which Saxons used but which Saxon craftsmen made no attempt to imitate or reproduce. At Sutton Hoo, however, the silver patches, one with Germanic birds' heads (*29*), and the garnets in the eyes of the boars' heads (*4*), tell us that the Saxon master-goldsmith repaired this great bowl himself, with pride and care, and using precious materials. When we then find incorporated in his marvellous jewellery, so full of new devices and ideas, *millefiori* glass chequers such as can be seen on two of the bowls (technically the simplest of the many *millefiori* themes represented) we recognize a clear instance, not merely of juxtaposition, but of creative fusion between the two traditions, Celtic and Anglo-Saxon. The jewellery already shows, in the first half of the seventh century, a Hiberno-Saxon, or more properly a Celto-Saxon, aspect.

The exotic things—Merovingian coins, the sixteen pieces of Eastern silver, the Coptic bowl from Alexandria, the Celtic bowls, the largest of them possibly having been made in Ireland, the Swedish treasures and heirlooms, and the intensive importation of garnets probably ultimately from India vividly illustrate the range of foreign contacts that could exist in an Anglo-Saxon royal court of the first half of the seventh century.

One cannot deal here with all the aspects of the ship-burial that have a special interest. The great drinking-horns, for example, are a vivid illustration of early Germanic life and custom, and of the evocative power of objects of daily life, on which the craftsmen expended their skills. The stringed instrument of music has attracted the attention of the students of Saxon poetry, for poetry was recited to the sounds of the lyre.[109] The reconstruction of a contemporary instrument, found in a courtly setting, must have relevance to the metric problems of the poetry, and may help to re-create its mood, its effect upon the listener, even the creative process itself. The intactness of the burial is important, not only because so much more is preserved than if it had been robbed, but because the grave-inventory is complete, and the full extent and nature of what it was thought fit to do can be seen. The objects in the burial are not ordinary, but in most instances startlingly novel and in some unique. Here once more horizons widen. Again, the burial has yielded examples of craftsmanship at the highest level yet encountered. Everything, including the Swedish pieces, is of this quality. The helmet is richer than any of its class yet found in Sweden, and differs in some ways from all of them. The shield is much richer and more elaborate than any of its Swedish counterparts, as its final revised reconstruction shows (*19*). We are here encountering such Swedish objects also for the first time at the royal level. The ship itself, relatively closely dated, is a landmark in the history of boat-construction. A hundred other features of the burial are of prime importance to the specialist. A great deal depends upon acceptance of the new date, for in this much of the interpretation and significance of the material will depend. But enough has been said to explain, and, I believe, justify, Sir Thomas Kendrick's description of the burial as 'the most marvellous find in the archaeological annals of England', and to make clear once again the depth of the Nation's debt of gratitude to the late Edith May Pretty, to whom the country owes one of the most remarkable and splendid gifts ever received by the national archaeological collections in a donor's life-time.

NOTES

1 For full details see R. L. S. Bruce-Mitford, 'Excavations at Sutton Hoo in 1938', *Proceedings of the Suffolk Institute of Archaeology*, vol. XXX, 1964, pp. 1–43.

2 A glass bowl of this type from a barrow at Broomfield, Essex, is normally exhibited with the Anglo-Saxon antiquities.

3 Professor W. F. Grimes did the main and most critical work in dissecting and removing the burial deposit. Professor Stuart Piggott and Mrs Margaret Guido also worked on the excavation and planning of the burial deposit. Professor Grahame Clark, Dr J. B. Ward-Perkins, and Mr J. W. Brailsford were also present at times, and lent advice or took valuable photographs. Dr O. G. S. Crawford, the Archaeology Officer of HM Ordnance Survey, and founder-Editor of *Antiquity*, made a fine photographic record of the excavation of the burial deposit on 25, 26 and 27 July. A most valuable and comprehensive record of the ship (five hundred and seventy-three negatives) was made by two amateur photographers then holidaying in Woodbridge (Miss M. Lack, ARPS and Miss B. Wagstaff, ARPS).

4 For the Oseberg and Gokstad ships see A. W. Brøgger and Haakon Shetelig, *The Viking Ships*, Oslo, 1951. This has no bibliography, but one is to be found in the Norwegian original edition of 1950. The definitive account of the Oseberg burial is *Osebergfundet* by Haakon Shetelig, Kristiania, 1917 and 1920. Good recent pictures and discussion of the Oseberg and Gokstad ships are to be found in *The Vikings* (chief contributor Professor Bertil Almgren), London, 1966.

5 Knud Thorvildsen, *Ladbyskibet*, København, 1957.

6 As suggested to me by Professor Sune Lindqvist of Uppsala University.

7 Lines 1020–45: Beowulf is given a 'gilded ensign, a decorated battle banner' (Clark Hall's translation) or 'a gold standard in meed of victory, chased, with a hilt' (Gavin Bone's modern verse translation): the Old English reads '*segen gyldenne . . . hroden hildecumbor*' (lines 1021–2, Klaeber, 3rd ed., 1941) with the variant readings of *hiltecumbor* in line 1022 (manuscript reading) or *hiltcumbor* (ed. M. Trautman, 1904).

8 Lines 2767–71: 'hanging high above the hoard a standard all of gold, greatest of marvels wrought by hand, woven by human skill' (Clark Hall)

> *segn eallgylden*
> *heah ofer horde, hondwundra maest*
> *gelocen leodocraeftum*

9 *Ecclesiastical History*, bk. II, ch. xvi: 'He had such excellence of glory in the kingdom that not only in battle were banners borne before him, but, in time of peace too, a standard-bearer' (*signifer*) 'was accustomed to go before him whensoever he rode about the cities, townships or shires with his thegns; yea, even when he passed through the streets to any place there was wont to be carried before him that kind of banner' (*vexillum*) 'which the Romans call Tufa, but the English Tuuf' (ed. J. E. King, Loeb edition, 1930).

10 For this royal site no doubt connected with the Sutton Hoo burial see R. L. S. Bruce-Mitford, 'Saxon Rendlesham', *Proceedings of the Suffolk Institute of Archaeology*, vol. XXIV, 1948, pp. 228–51.

11 For extensive discussions see *Herrschaftszeichen und Staatssymbolik* by P. E. Schramm, Bd. 1, 1954; K. Hauck, 'Halsring und Ahnenstab als herrscherliche Würdezeichen, III, Das Steinszepter von Sutton Hoo' (pp. 260–80). See also Sidney L. Cohen, 'The Sutton Hoo Whetstone', *Speculum*, July 1966, pp. 466–70.

12 Two of these objects, both normally exhibited among the late Celtic antiquities in the Museum, are illustrated in R. L. S. Bruce-Mitford, 'The Sutton Hoo ship-burial: recent theories and some comments on general interpretation', *Proceedings of the Suffolk Institute of Archaeology*, vol. XXV, 1949, p. 58, plates V and VI. That from Lochar Moss (in the Dumfries Museum) is as yet unpublished. For the one from Hough-on-the-Hill (in Lincoln Museum) see D. F. Petch, 'Archaeological notes for 1956, no. 25', *Lincolnshire Architectural and Archaeological Society, Reports and Papers*, vol. VII, 1957, pp. 17–19, plate II, figure 4.

13 Mr Herbert Maryon's paper on the shield in *Antiquity*, vol. XX, 1946, pp. 21–30, some of which is rendered obsolete by recent work.

14 For parallels see G. Arwidsson, *Valsgärde 8*, Uppsala, 1954, plates 10 and 11.

15 Rings were attached to the pommels of swords to denote and symbolize high rank or status. Ring-swords are therefore uncommon. At first loose and open, rings later became solid, functionless and, in Scandinavia, sometimes of enormous size. A ring-sword pommel from Italy with the ring in position is normally to be seen on exhibition among the Continental Germanic material. For further information see H. R. Ellis Davidson, *The Sword in Anglo-Saxon England*, Oxford, 1962, pp. 71–6 *et passim*, and V. I. Evison, in *Archaeologia*, vol. CI, 1967, pp. 63–118, especially pp. 71–2, 77 and 91.

16 Boat-grave 7 at Valsgärde, G. Arwidsson, *Välsgärde 7*, Uppsala, 1977.

17 The best reproductions of this sword-hilt are to be found in *Meddelanden från Lunds Universitetets Historiska Museum*, 1950, p. 145, figure 6 (H. Arbman, 'Verroterie cloisonnée et filigrane'). A drawing was published by Oscar Montelius in *The Civilization of Sweden in Heathen Times*, p. 135, figure 138. See also Elis H. Behmer, *Das zweischneidige Schwert des germanischen Völkerwanderungszeit*, Stockholm, 1939, plate XLII, 2. A fine photograph also appears in the German version of the *Catalogue of the Exhibition of Swedish Gold*, plate 21.

18 H. Stolpe and T. J. Arne, *La nécropole de Vendel*, Stockholm, 1927.

19 Similar bronze bowls, and one from the Taplow barrow (Buckinghamshire) with a pedestal foot (see *Victoria County History, Buckinghamshire*, vol. I, p. 202) are normally to be seen on display with the Anglo-Saxon collections. These bowls, known as 'Coptic bowls', apart from the occasional local imitation, are believed to have been manufactured in Alexandria. They occur in rich Germanic burials in north Italy, south Germany, the middle Rhineland and south-east England.

20 Other Celtic hanging-bowls, some with enamelled escutcheons, are normally to be seen on exhibition in the Museum. The Lullingstone bowl, perhaps the work of a Saxon craftsman, is especially noteworthy. Their function is uncertain. They are generally thought to have been designed for use in the Christian churches of the Celtic west, and to have come for the most part into the hands of the pagan Saxon invaders as loot.

21 For the Oberflacht lyre see Peter Paulsen, *Das alamannische Gräberfeld von Oberflacht*, vol. II, pp. 411–35, and for a discussion of early Germanic lyres and harps, Rupert and Myrtle Bruce-Mitford, 'The Sutton Hoo lyre, Beowulf and the origins of the Frame Harp', *Antiquity*, XLIV, March 1970, pp. 7–13. See also note 109 below.

22 A fragmentary iron tailpiece was found with the lyre in the eighth-century grave at St Severin's Church, Cologne—F. Fremersdorf, Zwei Wichtige Frankengräber aus Köln, *IPEK* (*Jahrbuch für prähistorische und ethnographische Kunst*), 15. and 16. Band, 1941–42, pp. 136–7, plates 49, 55, 56. Its design—a curved, waisted shape with an oval top—conforms with that of the instrument to which it belonged, and cannot therefore be taken as a reliable guide to the shape of the Sutton Hoo tailpiece, which belonged to a straight-sided, untapered instrument.

23 For early (pre-tenth century) niello, see Dr A. A. Moss, FSA, in *Studies in Conservation*, vol. II, 1953, pp. 49–62; and his note in *Antiquaries Journal*, vol. XXXIII, 1953, pp. 75–7.

24 The earlier reconstruction by Mr Herbert Maryon has been made obsolete by recent work. For Maryon's own account see *Antiquity*, vol. XXI, 1947, pp. 137–144.

25 Drinking-horns with silver-gilt mounts from the burial-mound at Taplow, in Buckinghamshire, the richest Anglo-Saxon grave known prior to the Sutton Hoo discovery, one in glass from Rainham, Essex, and others in glass from a Frankish grave and from

Italy are normally on exhibition with the Anglo-Saxon and early Teutonic collections, and may be compared with the pair from Sutton Hoo.

26 From the Taplow barrow: *Victoria County History, Buckinghamshire*, vol. I, p. 202; N. Åberg, *The Anglo-Saxons in England*, Uppsala, 1926, figure 1 (4) and figures 2 and 3.

27 E.g. Farthing Down, Surrey (E. T. Leeds, *Early Anglo-Saxon Art and Archaeology*, p. 65, figure 15) and Broomfield, Essex, *Proceedings of the Society of Antiquaries*, 2nd series, vol. XV, 1894, p. 252.

28 For this and the following quotations see *Runes: an introduction* by Ralph W. V. Elliott, Manchester University Press, 1959, pp. 46–51.

29 A similar vessel in the fourth-century treasure of Roman silver found at Mildenhall, Suffolk, is on view in the Roman Britain Room. The soldered handles of the Sutton Hoo dish had become detached from it and were at first thought to belong to a supposed leather bag found underneath it.

30 *Victoria County History, Essex*, vol. I, 1903, p. 323. See R. Cornwallis Neville 'Description of a remarkable deposit of Roman antiquities of iron, discovered at Great Chesterford, Essex, in 1854', *Archaeological Journal*, vol. XIII, pp. 4–5, plate 3, and S. Piggott, 'Three metal-work hoards of the Roman period from southern Scotland', *Proceedings of the Society of Antiquaries of Scotland*, vol. LXXXVII, 1952–53, pp. 1–50.

31 E.g. amongst the Vendel finds. The best analogy in this country is that from Great Chesterford in the Museum of Archaeology and Ethnology at Cambridge, an undated find assumed hitherto to be Romano-British. For Viking contexts, examples occur in boat-graves of this period at Valsgärde and in the Oseberg ship.

32 Formerly mis-identified as a *scramasax*, the name given to single-edged knives and swords of distinctive shape commonly found from the seventh century onwards.

33 See H. Barker, in *Nature*, vol. 166, August, 1950, p. 348.

34 No instance is known to Germanic archaeology of the remains of a cremated body being interred with unburnt grave-goods laid out as for the inhumation rite. The boat-grave of the eighth century found at Lackalänge, in south-west Sweden in 1858 (Sune Lindqvist, 'Från Skånes Vendeltid,' *Från Stenålder til Rokoko, Studier tillägnade Otto Rydbeck*, Lund, 1937, pp. 103–11) was formerly thought to be an instance; but scrutiny of the original accounts of the excavations makes it clear that it was not, as Lindqvist demonstrates. Such a mixing of radically opposed concepts would have to be regarded as freakish, and conceivable here only in the freakish context of Raedwald, a lapsed Christian who is known to have tried to ensure the best of both worlds by setting up side by side in his temple altars dedicated to Christ and the Devil (presumably Woden) (Bede, *Ecclesiastical History*, bk. II, ch. xv). But such an explanation of chemical traces is speculation, not susceptible of proof. Many factors, including the date that may be finally established of the other burials, and the incidence of inhumation and cremation in the grave field at Sutton Hoo, which can be established only when the whole site is excavated, are relevant to the problem. Instances from the Viking period (ninth/eleventh centuries AD) are known where burnt animal bones were scattered over inhumations, in association with human sacrifice (suttee) (G. Bersu and D. M. Wilson, *Three Viking graves in the Isle of Man*, Society for Medieval Archaeology Monograph Series, no. 1, 1966, pp. 10, 51, and *passim*).

35 In *Antiquaries Journal*, vol. XX, 1940, p. 172, C. W. Phillips records the discovery of what is the best-preserved of the presumed gaming-pieces under the Anastasius dish, saying that no traces of others were seen. The material from the burial-deposit, however, is now found to have contained fragments of several more pieces apparently identical and similarly impregnated with copper salts from adjacent bronze. These further pieces were in boxes whose number indicate that they came from the perimeter of the shield, at the west end of the deposit. The best-preserved gaming-piece is recorded by Sir Thomas Kendrick in his Inventory appended to Mr Phillips' *Antiquaries Journal* report vol. LXXX, p. 196.

36 For example, the Queen's ship-burial at Oseberg (about AD 800). The practice is also described in the well-known description by the Arabic writer, Ibn Fadlan, of the cremation in a funeral ship on the banks of the Volga of a Swedish Viking chieftain. (T. D. Kendrick, *History of the Vikings*, 1930, p. 159; *Antiquity*, vol. VIII, 1934, p. 58.) Excavations during the war by Dr Gerhard Bersu in the Isle of Man revealed layers of cremated animal bones spread over mounds that contained inhumed human primary burials. (G. Bersu and D. M. Wilson, op. cit.) The Ladby ship (see note 5) held skeletal remains of eleven horses and at least four dogs.

37 As *66* shows, the mound was originally round like all the others. Its original shape has been determined in the excavations conducted in 1967–69 by Paul Ashbee.

38 The clay basin found high above the burial, formerly supposed to have ritual significance (*Antiquaries Journal*, vol. XX, plate XVIIa) is now known to be simply a natural formation.

39 The evidence from the 1939 excavations was not in itself conclusive, and we now depend chiefly on the interpretation of photographs taken by Miss M. Lack and Miss B. Wagstaff and also by Mr Phillips. The identification of gunwale spikes (which are taken as implying the presence of thole-bases) between ribs 3 and 4 forward and 22 and 23 aft seems clear, and analogy with all the other early ships of the era, from Nydam to Gokstad, would support the presence of oars in this position forward (between ribs 3 and 4).

40 Fully described by the present writer in 'The Snape boat-grave', *Proceedings of the Suffolk Institute of Archaeology*, vol. XXVI, 1952, 1–26.

41 T. D. Kendrick, *Anglo-Saxon Art to A.D. 900*, 1938, pp. 47, 48.

42 R. L. S. Bruce-Mitford, 'A new wooden ship's figure-head found in the Scheldt at Moerzeke-Mariekerke', *Acta Archaeologica*, vol. XXXVIII, 1967, pp. 199–209.

43 Although at Sutton Hoo personal ornaments were absent from the grave. The gold jewellery has more the character of a ceremonial outfit, i.e. of regalia.

44 *Beowulf*, translated by Kevin Crossley-Holland and introduced by Bruce Mitchell, published by Macmillan, in September 1968.

45 Scyld, whose funeral is here described, first came amongst his people as a foundling, abandoned in an open boat with only a sheaf of corn. When he died, the gifts placed in his funeral ship were of course incomparably greater. The passage illustrates the device of understatement common in Old English poetry. It is like describing the Sutton Hoo treasure as 'not a whit less valuable' than a sheaf of corn. (See Gavin Bone, *Beowulf in Modern Verse*, 1945, p. 16, note 1.)

46 Translation by Kevin Crossley-Holland, see note 44.

47 When objects are declared (by Coroner's jury) to be Treasure Trove, they become Crown property. If the Crown decides to retain them, they are usually assigned to a national museum, and the finder, provided that he has promptly declared his discovery and not caused damage to the objects, receives a money payment of their full market value. If the Crown does not wish to retain the objects, they become the property of the finder. Only objects of gold and silver (whether coin, bullion or plate) can be found to be Treasure Trove, and it is the finder (as declared by the Coroner's jury), not the landowner, who receives the money payment if they are so found.

48 M. Maurice Prou, *Les Monnaies mérovingiennes* (Catalogue des Monnaies Françaises de la Bibliothèque Nationale) Paris, 1892. A. de Belfort, *Description générale des monnaies mérovingiennes par ordre alphabétique des ateliers, publiée d'après les notes manuscrites de M. le Vicomte de Ponton d'Amécourt*, tomes I–V, Paris, 1892–95.

49 The position was set out in two papers in *Antiquity*, vol. XXVI, 1952, pp. 76–86, by Professor Philip Grierson and the present writer.

50 J. Lafaurie, 'Le Trésor d'Escharen', *Revue Numismatique*, VIe série, tome II, Paris, 1960, pp. 153–209.

51 See bibliography No. 23, p. 134.

52 Joachim Werner, *Das Alamannische Fürstengrab von Wittislingen*, Munich, 1950, pp. 52–7, for a discussion of purses in Germanic graves.

53 *Antiquity*, vol. XLIV, March 1970, pp. 14–18.

54 I am indebted to Dr J. P. C. Kent for confirmation of this impression in so far as the continental material is concerned.

55 P. Grierson, op. cit., and 'A stray from the Crondall hoard', in *Numismatic Chronicle*, 1953, pp. 148–9; C. H. V. Sutherland, *Anglo-Saxon Gold Coinage in the light of the Crondall hoard*, Oxford, 1948.

56 H. M. Chadwick, 'Who was he?', *Antiquity*, vol. XIV, 1940, pp. 76–87. R. L. S. Bruce-Mitford, 'The Sutton Hoo ship-burial: recent theories and some comments on general interpretation', *Proceedings of the Suffolk Institute of Archaeology*, vol. XXV, 1950, pp. 4–20, 40–3, 72–8. Revised in *Aspects of Anglo-Saxon Archaeology*, 1974.

57 See note 56 and especially pp. 4–20 of the paper cited. Also R. H. Hodgkin, *A History of the Anglo-Saxons*, 3rd ed., 1952, Appendix, pp, 696–734, on the Sutton Hoo ship-burial, especially p. 712. Professor Wallace-Hadrill, in warning against too confident an interpretation of the evidence for the royalty of the Sutton Hoo grave (J. M. Wallace-Hadrill, 'The graves of kings, an historical note on some archaeological evidence', *Studi medioevali*,

3 series, I, 1, Spoleto, Centro Italiano di Studi sull'alto Medioevo, 1960) disagrees with H. M. Chadwick (op. cit.) on the concentration of wealth at this time in royal hands, and (in the writer's view) steadily underestimates the archaeological case. No individual argument may be in itself conclusive, but the cumulative effect does not seem to be sufficiently appreciated.

58 As for example the Taplow barrow (British Museum) and such continental chieftains' graves as those at Morken, Beckum, Wittislingen, Krefeld-Gellep, and the princely graves, male and female, of Cologne and St Denis (the latter probably of the Frankish queen, Arnegundis).

59 Sune Lindqvist, *Uppsala Högar och Ottarshögen*, Stockholm, 1936 (with English summary). For Childéric's grave, discovered in 1653, the standard reference is the Abbé Cochet, *Le Tombeau de Childéric Ier*, Paris, 1859, a critical appraisal of the primary account in Latin published by J. J. Chifflet in 1655. Most of the treasure was stolen from the Cabinet des Médailles in 1831. A further basic work is that of E. Babelon, 'Le tombeau de Roi Childéric et les origines de l'orfèverie cloisonnée', *Mémoires de la Société Nationale des Antiquaires de France*, tome LXXVI, 1924, pp. 1–112.

60 Cf. also on this the views of Dr Ortwin Gamber, 'The Sutton Hoo military equipment— an attempted reconstruction', in *Journal of the Arms and Armour Society*, vol. V, no. 6, 1966, pp. 265–92.

61 For the question of the pagan or Christian character of the grave or cenotaph, see the present writer's paper, 'Recent theories' (note 56), pp. 20–43.

62 Chadwick, op. cit., pp, 80–1.

63 Some at least of the other mounds contained cremations (p. 15).

64 The genealogy as drawn up in this table incorporates the corrections suggested by Sir Frank Stenton, 'The East Anglian kings of the seventh century' in *The Anglo-Saxons. Studies presented to Bruce Dickins*, edited by P. Clemoes, Cambridge, 1959, pp. 43–52, but follows Mrs Sandra Glass in regarding the Aethelric, whose son and grandson (according to the most authoritative document, the late eighth- or earlier ninth-century Cotton manuscript) were to succeed to the throne, as more likely to be the elder, not the younger, brother of Anna; and as one and the same person as the Ecgric mentioned by Bede, who was a relative (*cognatus*) of Sigeberht, and co-ruler with him. Sigeberht was brother or half-brother to Eorpwald (Stenton, op. cit., p. 49, note 2) and so a son or step-son of Raedwald. It would be natural for him, the last of Raedwald's sons, to hand over the kingdom, when he became a monk, to Eni's eldest son, his cousin. When Sigeberht was brought out of his monastic retirement to join Ecgric (=Aethelric) in leading the East Anglian army in the field against the threat of Penda of Mercia, the two cousins (if we can accept this as the relationship) were both killed (soon after AD 640). The succession passed to Anna and from him in turn to his younger brothers Aethelhere and Aethewald, finally reverting, it is suggested, to the son of Aethelric (=Ecgric), the eldest of the four brothers. This son, Aldwulf, reigned for about forty-nine years, dying in 713. The two earliest genealogies of the East Anglian kings to survive, that in the Cotton manuscript (late eighth or early ninth century) and that in the *Historia Brittonum* (originally compiled probably in the early ninth century) respectively give the name of that son of Eni who was father of Aldwulf as Ethilric and as Edric. Stenton (op. cit.) takes the Edric of the latter as being a miscopying of Ethilric. Dr Kenneth Sisam, however, in his 'Anglo-Saxon royal genealogies', *Proceedings of the British Academy*, vol. XXXIX, 1953, pp. 287–348, maintains that the genealogy in the *Historia Brittonum* has an earlier source than the Vespasian genealogy. It seems possible to take the Edric which appears in it as an independent version of the name, and as the same as the Ecgric mentioned in Bede. On the death of Sigeberht and Ecgric, together in battle, the succession would, it is suggested, have passed over Aldwulf, as an infant, going to his three uncles in turn, before returning to him, the son of the eldest brother. If Ethilric and Ecgric are *not* to be taken as the same person, Ethilric would probably be a younger brother, Eni's youngest son, as Stenton suggests. The proposal to equate Ethilric and Edric with Ecgric was first made by Mrs Sandra Glass in her paper, 'The Sutton Hoo ship-burial', in *Antiquity*, vol. XXXVI, 1962, pp. 179–83, in which she advocates the claims of Ecgric as the person for whom the Sutton Hoo burial was carried out.

65 Mabillon, *Acta Sanctorum Ordinis S. Benedicti* (1734 ed.), III (1), p. 3. I am grateful to Mr J. L. N. O'Loughlin for this reference.

66 Cf. Chadwick, op. cit. p. 82, fn 9.

67 For Rendlesham and the possible church and temple there, see the present writer's 'Saxon

Rendlesham' in *Proceedings of the Suffolk Institute of Archaeology*, vol. XXIV, 1948, pp. 230 *et seq.*

68 Bede, *Ecclesiastical History*, bk. III, ch. xxiv.

69 Exhibited in the Roman Britain Room.

70 Wilhelm Levison in his Ford Lectures, *England and the Continent in the 8th century* (1943), pp. 7, 8, gives particulars of Frankish annual fairs and markets patronized by Saxon traders, in particular one established at St Denis, near Paris, in 634, where Saxons are singled out for special mention amongst the traders of various nations. 'We may imagine that at such gatherings the so-called "Coptic" bronze vessels found in Saxon graves were acquired by English traders, and conjecture a similar source for silver objects such as those discovered in 1939 in the Sutton Hoo ship-burial.'

71 E.g. Bede, bk. I, ch. xxxii; bk. II, chs. x and xi. For Ittenheim, see J. Werner *Der Fund von Ittenheim; ein alamannisches Fürstengrab des 7. Jahrhunderts im Elsass*, Strassburg, 1943. For Krefeld-Gellep, see R. Pirling, 'Ein fränkisches Fürstengrab aus Krefeld-Gellep', *Germania*, vol. XLII, 1964, pp. 188–216.

72 'He drew his designs as best as he could without troubling to co-ordinate the ornaments in the centre with those in the two outer rings. The eight-pointed star and the bird in the roundel lie unhappily at an oblique angle to the radii formed by the medallions of the border friezes. These radii themselves do not form right angles with each other. The execution of details also shows signs of untidiness' (E. Kitzinger, in his paper on the silver, *Antiquity*, vol. XIV, 1940, pp. 40–63, on which this account is based.) For the Control Stamps on the Anastasius dish see E. Cruikshank Dodd, *Byzantine Silver Stamps*, Dumbarton Oaks, Washington, 1961, pp. 6 ff.

73 Normally exhibited in the Roman Britain Room.

74 The seventh is badly buckled at one edge. The eighth and ninth are in fragments, and the tenth was entirely reduced to silver chloride.

75 Normally on exhibition with the Early Christian and Byzantine antiquities.

76 R. E. Kaske, 'The Silver Spoons of Sutton Hoo', *Speculum*, vol. XLII, 1967, pp. 670–2. The same suggestion had been made to me independently by Mr David Sherlock, and subsequently expanded in a paper by him in *Speculum*, vol. XLVII, 1972.

77 See p. 58.

78 Fine examples are normally to be seen on exhibition amongst the Anglo-Saxon antiquities.

79 There is no instance in the Sutton Hoo gold jewellery of *champlevé* technique (i.e. stones, or enamel, sunk in solid metal).

80 Hanging-bowls from Lullingstone, Kent, Winchester and Loveden Hill, Lincs and escutcheons from other bowls are normally exhibited. The finest of all the early bowls is the largest of the three found at Sutton Hoo, and this shows extensive use of *millefiori* glass inlays.

81 Cf. H. Stolpe and T. J. Arne, *La nécropole de Vendel*, Stockholm, 1927, plate VII, figures, 5, 6, 7, also plate I.

82 Filigree: 'jewel work of a delicate kind made with threads and beads, usually of gold and silver' (*Oxford English Dictionary*).

83 This had perished, and is replaced in the exhibited reconstructed purse-lid by plastic padding. The condition of the gold rivets at the back of the plaques indicated that they had been fastened into some substance harder than wood.

84 A Frankish open-work bronze mount, from Amiens, bearing this subject with lions erect, is normally exhibited with the foreign Teutonic material.

85 Figured in *Vendel i Fynd och Forskning*, Uppsala, 1938, figure 9; Knut Stjerna, *Essays on Beowulf*, Viking Club, 1912, figure 4; and Falk and Shetelig, *Scandinavian Archaeology*, Cambridge, 1937, plate 43, etc.

86 A very interesting parallel to these plaques is a jewelled cloisonné brooch from Reinstrup, now in the Copenhagen Museum. See 'Recent theories', *Proceedings of the Suffolk Institute of Archaeology*, vol. XXV, 1949, Plate IXa, p. 55 and figure 10. See pp. 43–72 of this paper for a full discussion of the Swedish connection at Sutton Hoo.

87 The name given to the products of the great school of art that flourished in the north of England in the late seventh and eighth centuries, the result of a fusion of Celtic, Irish, Saxon and Mediterranean influences. The Lindisfarne Gospels (exhibited in the British Library, Reference Division) and the Book of Durrow (in Trinity College, Dublin) are leading examples of the *genre*.

88 For a theory as to the nature of the royal ceremonial harness or outfit, and the uses of the individual strap-mounts, buckles, etc., see Dr Ortwin Gamber, 'The Sutton Hoo mili-

tary equipment—an attempted reconstruction', *Journal of the Arms and Armour Society*, vol. V, 1966, pp. 265–89.

89 Boars' heads occasionally appear, e.g. on a silver bracelet from Faversham, Kent (normally exhibited), in cloisonné work on a brooch from Faversham ('Recent theories', Plate XIV*a* and figure 9). The boar theme occurs on the Sutton Hoo helmet (the boars' heads at the ends of the eyebrows) and frequently on Vendel-type helmets in Sweden, and on one of the four bronze dies from Torslunda, Öland (note 85). The finest Anglo-Saxon example is the boar figure in the full round on the crest of the Benty Grange helmet (Sheffield Museum), which was cleaned and studied in the British Museum.

90 See T. D. Kendrick, *Anglo-Saxon art to A.D. 900*, 1938, and R. F. Jessup, *Anglo-Saxon jewellery*, 1950.

91 For pattern-welding see H. R. Ellis Davidson, *The sword in Anglo-Saxon England*, Oxford 1962, ch. 1, 'The making of the sword', and Appendix A.

92 E. Behmer, *Das zweischneidige Schwert der germanischen Völkerwanderungszeit*, Stockholm, 1939, plate XLII, 2. See the present writer's paper 'Recent theories' (*Proceedings of the Suffolk Institute of Archaeology*, vol. XXV, plates XI–XIII).

93 Behmer, op. cit., plates XL, 1 and 2, and XLII, 1. These three, and the one first mentioned, are all in the Statens Historiska Museum, Stockholm.

94 *British Museum Quarterly*, vol. XIII, 1938–39, p. 117.

95 For the use of these pyramids see the works of H. R. Ellis Davidson and Dr Ortwin Gamber already quoted. Less elaborate examples from Broomfield, Essex and Selsey, Sussex are normally on exhibition in the Early Medieval Room.

96 The brooch is the one already cited as illustrating the boar's head theme (note 89), and is normally on exhibition. For the Swedish pyramid-fragment, see the present writer's 'Recent theories' paper, plate XIV*d*. Also Sune Lindqvist, *Uppsala Högar och Ottarshögen*, p. 179, figure 101, and Birgit Arrhenius. 'En nyfunnen svärdsknapp från Uppsala Västhög', *Fornvännen*, 1963, pp. 225–45, and figure 9, where the identification of the fragment as part of a pyramid is questioned, but not disproven. It remains highly probable in the writer's view.

97 Donkey's heads in the round were rendered at the ends of the pommel of the sword in Childeric's grave, and the Reinstrup brooch (note 86) in Copenhagen attempts a four-fold version of the man-and-monsters theme in cloisonné, but in a much more abstruse, short-hand and un-naturalistic manner.

98 The Swedish connection is most fully discussed by the present writer, 'Recent theories' (see note 56), pp. 43–78, and 'Sutton Hoo and Sweden', *Archaeological News Letter*, no. 2, May 1948, pp. 5–7; and Sune Lindqvist, 'Sutton Hoo and Beowulf', *Antiquity*; vol. XXII, 1948, pp. 131–40. See also notes 86 and 105, especially the reference to Mr J. L. N. O'Loughlin's paper in *Medieval Archaeology*.

99 *Aspects of Anglo-Saxon Archaeology*, pp. 53–5.

100 Among 1300 graves of the third–fourth century AD recently excavated by Professor Ole Klindt-Jensen at Slusegaard on Bornholm, some forty can be possibly considered as boat-graves. Of these most were half-boats. Only some six to eight were whole boats, and these averaged 5 m (16 or 17 ft) in length. Some of the boats, or half-boats, were upside-down over the burial, others the right way up, and with planks laid across, from gunwale to gunwale. The cemetery was on the beach. These are the earliest actual boat-graves known. Their contents, however, were meagre, and the full panoply of the ritual as seen in the seventh-century graves in Suffolk and Uppland is not there (*Skalk*, Aarhus, 1962, pp. 3–6). I am indebted to Ole Crumlin-Pedersen for this reference.

It is very doubtful whether certain finds of isolated rivets, or groups of rivets, in Norway and Kent, represent boat-graves, still less that they represent boat-inhumations. (Sune Lindqvist, 'Fuskhögar och falska bätgravar', *Tor*, 1958, pp. 101–12.) A rich cist grave recently excavated by Norwegian archaeologists at Westness in Orkney contained many rivets, but was not a boat-grave.

101 The identities of the Geats is still disputed. See Gwyn Jones, *A History of the Vikings*, Oxford, 1968, pp. 42–4, for a valuable discussion: and a recent work, *The Geats of Beowulf*, by Jane Acombe Leake, Wisconsin, 1967. An archaeologist can have little doubt about the correctness of R. W. Chambers' thesis, which I follow (see also note 105.)

102 What seems to be a clear case of a burial of an elderly woman in a small boat was recorded by Montelius in 1895 at Augerum in the Blekinge province of south-east Sweden. The finds, which were not rich, date the grave to the sixth century AD (Birgit Arrhenius, *Båtgraven från Augerum*, *Tor*, 1960, pp. 167–85).

103 *Antiquity*, vol. XXII, 1948, pp. 135 ff.

104 *Victoria County History of Suffolk*, vol. 1, p. 338. The dies are illustrated in E. T. Leeds, *Early Anglo-Saxon Art and Archaeology*, plate XVIIIe.

105 For the relevance of Sutton Hoo to Beowulf studies, see Sune Lindqvist, 'Sutton Hoo and Beowulf', *Antiquity*, vol. XXII, pp. 131–40 (translated from the Swedish in *Fornvännen* 1948, pp. 94–110); Rosemary J. Cramp, '*Beowulf* and Archaeology', *Medieval Archaeology*, vol. I, 1957, pp. 57–77. Gösta Langenfelt, 'Beowulf och Fornsverige', *Ortnams Sällskapets i Uppsala Årskrift*, 1961, 1962 (with English summaries), underestimates the Swedish connection at Sutton Hoo and seeks to introduce the Swedish–Geatish material in Beowulf into England in Carolingian times via the English missions on the Continent. Some penetrating sentences of Dr Nora K. Chadwick, 'The Monsters and Beowulf' in *The Anglo-Saxons. Studies presented to Bruce Dickins*, ed. Peter Clemoes, 1959, pp. 202–3, may well be near the truth of the matter. See also Professor C. L. Wrenn's study, with many useful references, 'Sutton Hoo and Beowulf' reprinted in *An Anthology of Beowulf Criticism*, ed. Lewis E. Nicholson, Indiana, 1963, pp. 311–30, and the same author's supplement to the third edition of R. W. Chambers, *Beowulf, an Introduction to the Study of the Poem*. Cambridge, 1959 (reprinted 1963 and 1967), pp. 508–23. For the Scandinavian connections of the East Anglian royal geneaology, see J. L. N. O'Loughlin, 'Sutton Hoo—the evidence of the documents' in *Medieval Archaeology*, vol. VIII, 1964, pp. 1–19. For a study of the effect of the Sutton Hoo discovery on Ritchie Girvan's view of the background to the poem in Chapter III of his *Beowulf and the Seventh Century*, see the added chapter by Rupert Bruce-Mitford in the reissue of Girvan's book in 1971 (London), pp. 85–98.

106 T. D. Kendrick, *Anglo-Saxon art to A.D. 900*, 1938, pp. 190–1. Taking as a typical example the Hardingstone disc-brooch, he writes: 'the cloisonné decoration is gone, the boss is now an ugly white lump, and the ornament is an evenly spread close interlace in low relief that completely covers and entirely dominates the roundel. The Kentish ribbon animal of the Crundale pommel' (on exhibition, see also *83c*), 'is here seen to be sinking back into a cold, flat, lifeless mesh.' There was nothing to suggest that in East Anglia, as we now know from Sutton Hoo, cloisonné work in the mid-seventh century was at the most brilliant ever seen in Europe, that animal style was in full flower, and novelty and originality of design and technical skill at a peak of achievement.

107 See T. D. Kendrick in *Burlington Magazine*, vol. LXXVII, 1940, p. 174 *et seq.*

108 Well exemplified in the Lindisfarne Gospels, permanently exhibited in the British Library, Reference Division.

109 The word used in Old English for the instrument mentioned in connection with the declamation of poetry and song is *hearpe*, which is always translated as 'harp'. However, the accumulation of archaeological evidence seems to show conclusively that the standard instrument at this time was the round lyre and that the European harp, as that instrument is defined by musicologists, was not evolved until the tenth century. The name *hearpe* and the verb *hearpan* were then transferred also to the new instrument which, like the lyre, was plucked. (See Rupert and Myrtle Bruce-Mitford, 'The Sutton Hoo lyre, Beowulf and the origins of the frame harp', referred to in note 21 above, and the Bibliography, p. 133, no. 7.)

BIBLIOGRAPHY

A short bibliography principally of books or articles directly connected with the Sutton Hoo ship-burial

1 Bruce-Mitford, R. L. S., 'Saxon Rendlesham', *Proceedings of the Suffolk Institute of Archaeology*, vol. XXIV, 1948, pp. 228–51.

2 Bruce-Mitford, R. L. S., 'The Sutton Hoo ship-burial. Recent theories and comments on general interpretation', *Proceedings of the Suffolk Institute of Archaeology*, vol. XXV, 1949, pp. 1–78.

3 Bruce-Mitford, R. L. S., 'The Snape boat-grave', *Proceedings of the Suffolk Institute of Archaeology*, vol. XXVI, 1952, pp. 1–26.

4 Bruce-Mitford, R. L. S., 'Sutton Hoo—a rejoinder', *Antiquity*, vol. XXVI, 1952, pp. 76–82.

5 Bruce-Mitford, R. L. S., 'Excavations at Sutton Hoo in 1938', *Proceedings of the Suffolk Institute of Archaeology*, vol. XXX, 1964, pp. 1–43.

6 Bruce-Mitford, R. L. S., 'Sutton Hoo Excavations, 1965–7', *Antiquity*, vol. XLII, 1968, pp. 36–9.

7 Bruce-Mitford, Rupert, and Bruce-Mitford, Myrtle, 'The Sutton Hoo lyre, Beowulf, and the origins of the frame-harp', *Antiquity*, vol. XLIV, 1970, pp. 7–13.

8 Bruce-Mitford, Rupert, *Aspects of Anglo-Saxon Archaeology*, London, 1974.

9 Bruce-Mitford, Rupert, and others, *The Sutton Hoo Ship-burial*, vol. I, 1975 (vol. II forthcoming 1978).

10 Chadwick, H. M., 'Who was he?', *Antiquity*, vol. XIV, 1940, pp. 76–87.

11 Cramp, Rosemary J., 'Beowulf and Archaeology', *Medieval Archaeology*, vol. I, 1957, pp. 57–77.

12 Gamber, O., 'The Sutton Hoo military equipment—an attempted reconstruction', *Journal of the Arms and Armour Society*, vol. V, no. 6, 1966, pp. 265–92.

13 Girvan, Ritchie, *Beowulf and the seventh century*, London, 1971, with chapter on Sutton Hoo and the background to Beowulf, by R. L. S. Bruce-Mitford.

14 Glass, Mrs S., 'The Sutton Hoo ship-burial', *Antiquity*, vol. XXXVI, 1962, pp. 179–93.

15 Green, Charles, *Sutton Hoo*, London, 1963.

16 Grierson, Philip, 'The dating of the Sutton Hoo coins', *Antiquity*, vol. XXVI, 1952, pp. 83–6.

17 Grierson, Philip, 'The purpose of the Sutton Hoo coins', *Antiquity*, vol. XLIV, 1970, pp. 14–18.

18 Grohskopf, Mrs Bernice, *The Treasure of Sutton Hoo*, New York, 1969.

19 Hodgkin, R. H., *A History of the Anglo-Saxons*, vol. II, (3rd edition, 1952); Appendix on the Sutton Hoo Ship-Burial and notes by R. L. S. Bruce-Mitford, pp. 696–734.

20 Kaske, R. E., 'The Silver Spoons of Sutton Hoo', *Speculum*, vol. XLII, pp. 670–2.

21 Kendrick, T. D. and others, 'The Sutton Hoo finds', *British Museum Quarterly*, vol. XIII, 1938–9, pp. 111–36.

22 Kent, J. P. C., 'Problems of Chronology in the 7th century Merovingian Coinage', *Cunobelin* XIII, 1967, pp. 24–30.

23 Kent, J. P. C., and Oddy, W. A., 'The dating of the Sutton Hoo coins', *Methods of Chemical and Metallurgical Investigations of Ancient Coinage*, ed. E. T. Hall and D. M. Metcalfe (Royal Numismatic Society Special Publication No. 8 London, 1972).

24 Lafaurie, J., 'Le Trésor d'Escharen', *Revue Numismatique*, 1960, pp. 153–209.

25 Lindquist, Sune, 'Sutton Hoo and Sweden' (translated from *Fornvännen* (1948) by R. L. S. Bruce-Mitford), *Antiquity*, vol. XXII, 1948, pp 131–40.

26 O'Loughlin, J. L. N., 'Sutton Hoo—the evidence of the documents', *Medieval Archaeology*, vol. VIII, 1964, pp. 1–19.

27 Phillips, C. W., 'The Excavation of the Sutton Hoo Ship-burial'; R. L. S. Bruce-Mitford (Ed.), *Recent Archaeological Excavations*, London, 1956, pp. 143–66.

28 Phillips, C. W., Kendrick, T. D., Kitzinger, E., Crawford, O. G. S., Grimes, W. E. and Chadwick, H. M.*, 'The Sutton Hoo Ship-burial', *Antiquity*, vol. XIV, 1940.

29 Phillips, C. W., 'The Sutton Hoo Ship-burial', *Antiquaries Journal*, vol. XX, 1940.

30 Wrenn, C. L., Supplement to the 3rd ed. of R. W. Chambers, *Beowulf, an Introduction to the Study of the Poem*, Cambridge, 1959 (reprinted 1963 and 1967), pp. 508–23.

31 Wrenn, C. L., 'Sutton Hoo and Beowulf', *An Anthology of Beowulf Criticism*, ed. Lewis E. Nicholson, Indiana, 1963, pp. 311–30.

*The article 'Who was he?' cited separately above.

The following observations on the above works may be useful. Nos. 21 and 28, both of 1940, are early surveys which, though outdated in some respects, retain much of interest. No. 29 by Mr Phillips is the basic account of the excavation, and No. 27, his more personal recollection of the occasion. No. 24 gives one of the fundamental expositions of the new chronology for Merovingian coinage, the effect of which, on Sutton Hoo is summarized in Ch. VI of the Handbook.

Mr Charles Green's attractive work (No. 15) contains much that is of interest, in particular his personal views about the settlement of East Anglia and the crossing of the North Sea by the Anglo-Saxon invaders.

Mrs Grohskopf's book (No. 18) gives a simple account for the general reader of the cultural background of the seventh century, as well as an account of the Sutton Hoo discovery.

R. H. Hodgkin's well-known *History of the Anglo-Saxons* (No. 19) gives an authoritative and fascinating presentation of Anglo-Saxon history from the beginning to the Norman Conquest. Its Appendix on Sutton Hoo is however now largely out of date.

No. 2 gives the fullest discussion hitherto of many of the issues raised by the burial.

No. 8, it should however be noted, incorporates up-to-date and amended versions of items 1–7 in the bibliography; it also contains other relevant matter including the first full account of the Benty Grange helmet.

The ground covered by most of the items in the bibliography is moreover covered in a definitive manner, as far as this is possible, in No. 9, the first volume of the British Museum's definitive publication, published in 1975. This volume deals with the site, the 1938 and 1939 excavations, the coins, the date of the burial, the cenotaph problem, the historical background, the ship and other matters. It includes the official inventory of the finds from the ship-burial but does not otherwise deal with the individual items in the deposit. These will be covered in volumes II and III.